Principles of Spiritual Growth

by Miles J. Stanford

BACK TO THE BIBLE
LINCOLN, NE 68501

615,000 printed to date—1997
(1170-216—5M—17)
ISBN 0-8474-0739-X

Printed in the United States of America

Foreword

A friend once handed me a copy of a book entitled *The Green Letters*, written by Miles J. Stanford. After reading the first few pages, I knew I had something in my hand that was extraordinary. Day by day during my devotional time I read at least one section and found the book to contain one of the most practical approaches to the various areas of my spiritual life that I have ever read. I asked others to read it, and they confirmed my impressions.

The various parts of the book were originally prepared as short letters and were sent to a number of interested friends. They were then compiled into the book that was known as *The Green Letters*, but in order to make this new printing meaningful to a new audience, the title has been changed to *Principles of Spiritual Growth*. We are thankful for permission from the author to publish this book for the benefit of a larger group of friends.

Set forth in this book are basic principles pertaining to the Christian's spiritual exercises. These principles are stated in such practical form that you will find it rewarding to read and reread them and, of course, to put them into practice. Some aspects of the Christian life and walk that may have been puzzling to you will become clear as the Spirit of God is able to make them a reality in your daily life.

While certain sections may be of such interest as to entice you to read them first, it would be best to read the sections in the order in which they appear. They are in a logical sequence, and precept is laid upon precept (Isa. 28:10). We trust there will be a wide distribution of these truths.

Theodore H. Epp
Founder
Back to the Bible

Contents

FAITH

The aim of this book is to carefully bring out some of the more important principles of spiritual growth in order to help build on a sound biblical foundation in Christ. He can honor no other.

The Holy Spirit had Paul write to each of us: "Examine yourselves, whether ye be in the faith" (II Cor. 13:5), and the recommendation is certainly not out of order at the very inception of this series of studies. First of all, we must remind ourselves that "without faith it is impossible to please him" (Heb. 11:6). Moreover, and this is all important, true faith must be based solely on scriptural *facts*, for "faith cometh by hearing, and hearing by the word of God" (Rom. 10:17). Unless our faith is established on facts, it is no more than conjecture, superstition, speculation or presumption.

Hebrews 11:1 leaves no question about this: "Faith is the substance of things hoped for, the evidence of things not seen." Faith standing on the facts of the Word of God substantiates and gives evidence of things not seen. And everyone knows that evidence must be founded on facts. All of us started on this principle when we were born again—our belief stood directly on the eternal fact of the redeeming death and resurrection of our Lord and Saviour Jesus Christ, as recorded in I Corinthians 15:1-4. This is the faith by which we began, and it is the same faith by which we are to "stand" (16:13), "walk" (II Cor. 5:7) and "live" (Gal. 2:20). "As ye have therefore received Christ Jesus the Lord, so walk ye in him" (Col. 2:6).

Since true faith is anchored on scriptural facts, we are certainly not to be influenced by *impressions*. George Mueller said, "Impressions have neither one thing nor the other to do with faith. Faith has to do with the Word of God. It is not impressions, strong or weak, which will make the difference. We have to do with the Written Word and not ourselves or our impressions."

Then, too, *probabilities* are the big temptation when it comes to exercising faith. Too often the attitude is: "It doesn't seem probable that he will ever be saved." "The way things are going, I wonder if the Lord really loves me." But Mueller wrote: "Many people are willing to believe regarding those things that seem probable to them. Faith has nothing to do with probabilities. The province of faith begins where probabilities cease and sight and sense fail. Appearances are not to be taken into account. The question is—whether God has spoken it in His Word."

Alexander R. Hay adds to this by saying, "Faith must be based upon *certainty*. There must be definite knowledge of God's purpose and will. Without that there can be no true faith. For faith is not a force that we exercise or a striving to believe that something shall be, thinking that if we believe hard enough it will come to pass." That may be positive thinking but certainly not biblical faith.

Evan Hopkins writes: "Faith needs facts to *rest* upon. Presumption can take fancy instead of fact. God in His Word reveals to us the facts with which faith has to deal." It is on this basis that J. B. Stoney can say, "Real faith is always increased by opposition, while false confidence is damaged and discouraged by it." There can be no steadfastness apart from immovable facts. Peter's burden was: "That the trial of your faith, being much more precious than of gold that perisheth, though it be tried with fire, might be found unto praise and honour and glory at the appearing of Jesus Christ" (I Pet. 1:7).

Once we begin to reckon (count) on facts, our Father begins to build us up in the faith. From his profoundly simple trust in God, Mueller was able to say that "God delights to increase the faith of His children. We ought, instead of wanting no trials before victory, no exercise for patience, to be willing to take them from God's hand as a means. I say— and say it deliberately—trials, obstacles, difficulties, and sometimes defeats, are the very food of faith."

On this same subject James McConkey wrote: "Faith is *dependence* upon God. And this God-dependence only begins when self-dependence ends. And self-dependence only comes to its end, with some of us, when sorrow, suffering, affliction, broken plans and hopes bring us to that place of self-helplessness and defeat. And only then do we find that we have learned the lesson of faith; to find our tiny craft of life rushing onward to a blessed victory of life and power and service undreamt of in the days of fleshly strength and self-reliance."

J. B. Stoney agrees by saying, "It is a great thing to *learn* faith: that is, simple dependence upon God. It will comfort you much to be assured that the Lord is teaching you dependence upon Himself, and it is very remarkable that faith is necessary in *everything*. 'The just shall live by faith,' not only in your circumstances, but in everything. I believe the Lord allows many things to happen on purpose to make us feel our need of Him. The more you find Him in your sorrows or wants, the more you will be attached to Him and drawn away from this place where the sorrows are, to Him in the place where He is." "Set your affection on things above" (Col. 3:2).

Actually, we cannot trust anyone further than we know him. So we must not only learn the facts involved but ever more intimately come to know the One who presents and upholds them! "And this is life eternal, that they might know thee the only true God, and Jesus Christ, whom thou hast sent" (John 17:3). "Grace and peace be multiplied unto you through the knowledge of God, and of Jesus our Lord, according as his divine power hath given unto us all things that pertain unto life and godliness, through the knowledge of him that hath called us to glory and virtue: whereby are given unto us exceeding great and precious promises: that by these ye might be partakers of the divine nature" (II Pet. 1:2-4).

TIME

It seems that most believers have difficulty in realizing and facing up to the inexorable fact that God does not hurry in His development of our Christian life. He is working from and for eternity! So many feel they are not making progress unless they are swiftly and constantly forging ahead. Now it is true that the new convert often begins and continues for some time at a fast rate. But this will not continue if there is to be healthy growth and ultimate maturity. God Himself will modify the pace. This is important to see, since in most instances when seeming declension begins to set in, it is not, as so many think, a matter of backsliding.

John Darby makes it plain that "it is God's way to set people aside after their first start, that self-confidence may die down. Thus Moses was forty years. On his first start he had to run away. Paul was three years also, after his first testimony. Not that God did not approve the first earnest testimony. We must get to know ourselves and that we have no strength. Thus we must learn, and then leaning on the Lord we can with more maturity, and more experientially, deal with souls."

Since the Christian life matures and becomes fruitful by the principle of growth (see II Pet. 3:18) rather than by struggle and "experiences," much time is involved. Unless we see and acquiesce to this, there is bound to be constant frustration, to say nothing of resistance to our Father's development processes for us. Dr. A. H. Strong illustrates for us: "A student asked the President of his school whether he could not take a shorter course than the one prescribed. 'Oh yes,' replied the President, 'but then it depends upon what you want to be. When God wants to make an oak, He takes a hundred years, but when He wants to make a squash, He takes six months.'" Strong also wisely points out to us that "growth is not a uniform thing in the tree or in the Christian. In some single months there is more growth than in all the year besides. During the rest of the year, however, there is solidification, without which the green timber would be useless. The period of rapid growth, when woody fibre is actually deposited between the bark and the trunk, occupies but four to six weeks in May, June and July."

Let's settle it once and for all—there are no shortcuts to reality! A meteor is on a shortcut as it proceeds to burn out, but not a star, with its steady light so often depended on by navigators. Unless the time factor is acknowledged from the heart, there is always danger of turning to the false enticement of a shortcut via the means of "experiences" and "blessings," where one becomes pathetically enmeshed in the vortex of ever-changing feelings, adrift from the moorings of scriptural facts.

In regard to this subject George Goodman writes: "Some have been betrayed into professing perfection or full deliverance, because at the time they speak they are happy and confident in the Lord. They forget that it is not a present experience that ensures fruit unto maturity, but a patient continuance in well doing. To taste of the grace of God is one thing; to be established in it and manifest it in character, habit, and regular life, is another. Experiences and blessings, though real gracious visitations from the Lord, are not sufficient to rest upon, nor should they lead us to glory in ourselves, as if we had a store of grace for time to come, or were yet at the end of the conflict. No. Fruit ripens slowly; days of sunshine and days of storm each add their share. Blessing will succeed blessing, and storm follow storm before the fruit is full grown or comes to maturity."

In that the Husbandman's method for true spiritual growth involves pain as well as joy, suffering as well as happiness, failure as well as success, inactivity as well as service, death as well as life, the temptation to shortcut is especially strong unless we see the value of, and submit to, the necessity of the time element. In simple trust we must rest in His hands, "being confident of this very thing, that he which hath begun a good work in you will perform it until the day of Jesus Christ" (Phil. 1:6). And it will take that long! But since God is working for eternity, why should we be concerned about the time involved?

Graham Scroggie affirmed, "Spiritual renewal is a gradual process. All growth is progressive, and the finer the organism, the longer the process. It is from measure to measure: thirtyfold, sixtyfold, an hundredfold. It is from stage to stage: 'first the blade, then the ear, and after that, the full corn in the ear.' And it is from day to day. How varied these are! There are great days, days of decisive battles, days of crises in spiritual history, days of triumph in Christian service, days of the right hand of God upon us. But there are also idle days, days apparently useless, when even prayer and holy service seem a burden. Are we, in any sense, renewed in these days? Yes, for any experience which makes us more aware of our need of God must contribute to spiritual progress, unless we deny the Lord who bought us."

We might consider some familiar names of believers whom God obviously brought to maturity and used for His glory—such as Pierson, Chapman, Tauler, Moody, Goforth, Mueller, Taylor, Watt, Trumbull, Meyer, Murray, Havergal, Guyon, Mabie, Gordon, Hyde, Mantle, McCheyne, McConkey, Deck, Paxson, Stoney, Saphir, Carmichael and Hopkins. The average for these was 15 years after they entered their life work before they began to know the Lord Jesus as their Life and ceased trying to work for Him and began allowing Him to be their All in all and do His work through them. This is not to discourage us in any way but to help us to settle down with our sights on eternity, by faith "apprehend[ing] that for which also . . . [we are] apprehended of Christ Jesus. . . . Press[ing] toward the mark for the prize of the high calling of God in Christ Jesus" (Phil. 3:12,14).

Certainly this is not to discount a Spirit-fostered experience, blessing, or even a crisis; but it is to be remembered that these simply contribute to the overall, and all-important, process. It takes time to get to know ourselves; it takes time and eternity to get to know our infinite Lord Jesus Christ. Today is the day to put our hand to the plow and to irrevocably set our heart on His goal for us—that we "may know him, and the power of his resurrection, and the fellowship of his sufferings, being made conformable unto his death" (v. 10).

"So often in the battle," says Austin-Sparks, "we go to the Lord, and pray, and plead, and appeal for victory, for ascendency, for mastery over the forces of evil and death, and our thought is that in some way the Lord is going to come in with a mighty exercise of power and put us into a place of victory and spiritual ascendency as in an act. We must have this mentality corrected. What the Lord does is to enlarge us to possess. He puts us through some exercise, through some experience, takes us by some way which means our spiritual expansion, and exercise of spirituality so we occupy the larger place spontaneously. 'I will not drive them out from before thee in one year; lest the land become desolate, and the beast of the field multiply against thee. By little and little I will drive them out before thee, until thou be increased' (Ex. 23:29,30).

"One day in the House of Commons, British Prime Minister Disraeli made a brilliant speech on the spur of the moment. That night a friend said to him, 'I must tell you how much I enjoyed your extemporaneous talk. It's been on my mind all day.' 'Madam,' confessed Disraeli, 'that extemporaneous talk has been on my mind for twenty years!' "

ACCEPTANCE

There are two questions that every believer must settle as soon as possible. The one is, Does God fully accept me? and the second, If so, upon what basis does He do so? This is crucial. What devastation often permeates the life of one, young or old, rich or poor, saved or unsaved, who is not sure of being accepted, even on the human level.

Yet so many believers, whether "strugglers" or "vegetators," move through life without this precious fact to rest and build on: "Having predestinated us unto the adoption of children by Jesus Christ to himself, according to the good pleasure of his will, to the praise of the glory of his grace, wherein he hath made us accepted in the beloved" (Eph. 1:5,6).

Every believer is accepted by the Father, in Christ. "Being justified by faith, we have peace with God through our Lord Jesus Christ" (Rom. 5:1). The peace is God's toward us, through His beloved Son—on this our peace is to be based. God is able to be at peace with us through our Lord Jesus Christ, "having made peace through the blood of his cross" (Col. 1:20). And we must never forget that His peace is founded solely on the work of the cross, totally apart from anything whatsoever in or from us, since "God commendeth his love toward us, in that, while we were yet sinners, Christ died for us" (Rom. 5:8).

Our faith becomes a fixed attitude once it begins to rest in this wonderful fact. Then it can be, if necessary, "disallowed [rejected] indeed of men, but chosen of God, and precious" (I Pet. 2:4). This is the steadying influence most believers are in need of today. A century ago J. B. Stoney wrote: "The blessed God never alters nor diverges from the acceptance in which He has received us because of the death and resurrection of Jesus Christ. Alas! we diverge from the state in which God can ever be toward us as recorded in Romans 5:1-11. Many suppose that because they are conscious of sins, hence they must renew their acceptance with God.

"The truth is that God has not altered. His eye rests on the work accomplished by Christ for the believer. When you are not walking in the Spirit you are in the flesh: you have turned to the old man which was crucified on the cross (Rom. 6:6). You have to be restored to fellowship, and when you are, you find your acceptance with God unchanged and unchangeable. When sins are introduced there is a fear that God has changed. He has not changed, but you have. You are not walking in the Spirit but in the flesh. You have to judge yourself in order to be restored. 'For this is my blood of the new testament, which is shed for many for the remission of sins' (Matt. 26:28). But if your sins are not met there, where can they be met? 'Now where remission of [sin] is, there is no more offering for sin' (Heb. 10:18). God has effected the reconciliation; He always remains true to it. Alas! We diverge from it; and the tendency is to suppose that the blessed God has altered toward us. He certainly will judge the flesh if we do not, but He never departs from the love which He has expressed to the prodigal, and we find that when the cloud, which walking in the flesh produced, has passed away, His love, blessed be His Name, had never changed."

God's basis must be our basis for acceptance. There is no other. We are "accepted in the beloved" (Eph. 1:6). Our Father is fully satisfied with His beloved Son on our behalf, and there is no reason for us not to be. Our satisfaction can only spring from and rest in His satisfaction. It is from God to us, not from us to God. J. N. Darby was very clear on this: "When the Holy Spirit reasons with man, He does not reason from what man is for God, but from what God is to man. Souls reason from what they are in themselves as to whether God can accept them. He cannot accept you thus; you are looking for righteousness in yourself as a ground of acceptance with Him. You cannot get peace whilst reasoning in that way.

"The Holy Spirit always reasons down from what God is, and this produces a total change in my soul. It is not that I abhor my sins; indeed I may have been walking very well; but it is 'I abhor myself.' This is how the Holy Spirit reasons; He shows us what we are, and that is one reason why He often seems to be very hard and does not give peace to the soul, as we are not relieved until we experientially, from our hearts, acknowledge what we are.

"Until the soul comes to that point He does not give it peace—He could not; it would be healing the wound slightly. The soul has to go on until it finds there is nothing to rest on but the abstract goodness of God; and then, 'If God be for us, who can be against us?' (Rom. 8:31)."

Sadly today, most believers actually reason just the opposite—from themselves to God. When all is going well and God seems to be blessing, then it is that they feel He loves and accepts them. But when they are stumbling and everything seems dry and hard, then they feel that He does not love and accept them. How can this be? There is nothing about us to commend us to God, our acceptance being in Christ, plus the fact that most of our true spiritual development comes through the dry and hard times. Thank God, He has accepted us in His Son, and upon this *fact* we must rest our faith. As in justification, our acceptance is by *grace* alone. In his classic, *Romans, Verse by Verse*, Wm. R. Newell presents some penetrating thoughts regarding this grace (pp. 245-47).

"There being no cause in the creature why Grace should be shown, the creature must be brought off from *trying to give cause* to God for His Grace.... He has been accepted *in Christ*, who *is* his standing! He is not 'on probation.' As to his life past, *it does not exist* before God: he *died* at the cross, and *Christ is his Life*. Grace, once bestowed, *is not withdrawn*: for God knew all the human exigencies beforehand: His action was independent of them, not dependent upon them....

"The Proper Attitude of Man Under Grace:

"To believe, and to consent to be *loved while unworthy*, is the great secret.

"To refuse to make 'resolutions' and 'vows'; for that is to trust in the flesh.

"To expect to be blessed, though realizing more and more lack of worth....

"To rely on God's chastening [child training] hand as a mark of His kindness....

"Things Which Gracious Souls Discover:

"To 'hope to be better' [hence acceptable] is to fail to see yourself *in Christ only*.

"To be *disappointed* with yourself, is to have *believed* in yourself.

"To be *discouraged* is *unbelief*,—as to God's purpose and plan of blessing for you.

"To be *proud*, is to be *blind*! For we have no standing before God, *in ourselves*.

"The lack of Divine blessing, therefore, comes from unbelief, and not from *failure of devotion*. . . .

"To preach devotion first, and blessing second, is to reverse God's order, and preach *law, not grace*. The Law made man's blessing depend on devotion; Grace *confers undeserved, unconditional* blessing: our devotion may follow, but does not always do so,—in proper measure."

Have we been afraid to really believe God? Have some even been afraid to allow others to really believe Him? We must never forget that "God's ways are not always man's ways. To some men constant peril is the only spur to action, and many religions and psychologies are dependent on fear to keep their disciples in line. Fear, too, has a place in Christianity, but God has higher and more effective motivations than fear, and one of these is love. Often fear after a while produces only numbness, but love thrives on love. To promise a man the certainty of his destiny may seem, on the human level, like playing with fire; but this leaves God out of the picture. Those who have the deepest appreciation of grace do not continue in sin. Moreover, fear produces the obedience of slaves; love engenders the obedience of sons" (J. W. Sanderson, Jr.).

"For if the trumpet give an uncertain sound, who shall prepare himself to the battle?" (I Cor. 14:8). Until the Christian is absolutely and scripturally sure of his standing, he is not going to do much standing. "Stand therefore" (Eph. 6:14).

"Now our Lord Jesus Christ himself, and God, even our Father, which hath loved us, and hath given us everlasting consolation and good hope through grace, comfort your hearts, and stablish you in every good word and work" (II Thess. 2:16,17).

PURPOSE

How wonderful and encouraging it is to know that our Heavenly Father has made it crystal clear in His Word exactly what His purpose is for each one of us. Now is the time, right in these next few moments, to make sure on the authority of His eternal Word, as to His purpose for your personal life.

"And God said, Let us make man in our image" (Gen. 1:26). The first Adam, the head of the human race, was made in God's image in the realm of personality, intellect, emotions, will, and so on, so that there could be communion, fellowship and cooperation between them; with God sovereign and man subject—subject to His will, which is perfect freedom. But we know that Adam chose his own way in preference to God's way, relying on himself only, loving just himself. As a result he immediately became self-centered instead of God-centered; dead to God who is the source of all life, dead in trespasses and sins. In this condition Adam "begat a son in his own likeness, after his [fallen] image" (Gen. 5:3). Thus he brought forth a sinful, ungodly, self-centered race, born "dead in trespasses and sins" (Eph. 2:1).

"God ... hath in these last days spoken unto us by his Son; ... who being the brightness of his glory, and the express image of his person" (Heb. 1:1-3). Here is the image of God back on earth, this time in the Person of our Lord Jesus Christ, God's "last Adam" (I Cor. 15:45). Our natural birth made us members of the fallen, sinful first-Adam race. Our transition from the old sinful race to the new godly race is known as the "new birth." When we were born again, through "repentance toward God, and faith toward our Lord Jesus Christ" (Acts 20:21), we were born into Him—He became our life (see Col. 3:3,4). "Thou wert cut out of the olive tree which is wild by nature, and wert graffed contrary to nature into a good olive tree" (Rom. 11:24). "For as by one man's [Adam's] disobedience many were made sinners, so by the obedience of one [Christ] shall many be made righteous" (5:19).

Our Heavenly Father is still carrying out His purpose of making man in His image. Although His original purpose is the same, He is not using the original man to bring it about. *All* is now centered in the Last Adam, our Lord Jesus. Being born into Him through faith, we became "partakers of the divine nature" (II Pet. 1:4). And as the Lord Jesus is allowed to express Himself through our personality, this poor, sin-sick world will see "Christ in you, the hope of glory" (Col. 1:27). In I Corinthians 15:49 Paul gives us the heartening promise: "As we have borne the image of the earthy [Adam], we shall also bear the image of the heavenly [Christ]."

"And we know that all things work together for good to them that love God, to them who are the called according to his purpose. For whom he did foreknow, he also did predestinate to be conformed to the image of his Son" (Rom. 8:28,29). Here is the "good" for which God is working all things together—His original purpose of making us in His image, which is centered and expressed in His Son, Christ who is our life. Paul's determination for each of his converts was: "My little children, of whom I travail in birth again until Christ be formed in you" (Gal. 4:19).

The open secret of healthy spiritual growth is to know and settle upon this fact as set forth in Romans 8:28,29. When we see that all things are working together to make us more and more like the Lord Jesus, we will not be frustrated and upset when some of these "things" are hard, difficult to understand, and often contain an element of death. We will be able to rest in our Lord Jesus and say to our Father, "Thy will be done." And our constant attitude of faith will be: "Though he slay me, yet will I trust in him" (Job 13:15). This is our matriculation to spiritual maturity!

"But we all, with open face beholding as in a glass the glory of the Lord, are changed into the same image from glory to glory, even as by the Spirit of the Lord" (II Cor. 3:18). It is one thing to know what God's purpose is for our lives, and it is another to know something of the "how" as to entering into it all right here and now. One of God's most effective means in the process is failure. Many believers are simply frantic over the fact of failure in their lives, and they will go to all lengths in trying to hide it, ignore it, or rationalize about it. And all the time they are resisting the main instrument in the Father's hand for conforming us to the image of His Son!

Failure where self is concerned in our Christian life and service is allowed and often engineered by God in order to turn us completely from ourselves to His source for our life—Christ Jesus, who never fails. We are to rejoice in our need and hunger of heart, for God says, "Blessed are they which do hunger and thirst after righteousness: for they shall be filled" (Matt. 5:6). As we, in our abject need, consistently and lovingly look upon our Lord Jesus, who is revealed to us in the Word, the Holy Spirit will quietly and effortlessly change the center and source of our lives from self to Christ—hence for each of us it will be "not I, but Christ" (Gal. 2:20).

God has a natural law in force to the effect that we are conformed to that on which we center our interest and love. Hawthorne brought out this fact in "The Great Stone Face." Then, too, think of Germany some years ago, full of little Hitlers all because of fanatical devotion to a second-rate paper hanger! Here in America radio, TV and movies contribute to a rising generation of young people who try to emulate their entertainment heroes. And what of the believer? If we are attracted to this present evil world, we become increasingly worldly; if we pamper and live for self, we become more and more self-centered; but when we look to Jesus Christ, we become more and more like Him.

Norman Douty writes: "If I am to be like Him, then God in His grace must do it, and the sooner I come to recognize it the sooner I will be delivered from another form of bondage. Throw down every endeavor and say, I cannot do it, the more I try the farther I get from His likeness. What shall I do? Ah, the Holy Spirit says, You cannot do it; just withdraw; come out of it. You have been in the arena, you have been endeavoring, you are a failure, come out and sit down, and as you sit there behold Him, look at Him. Don't try to be like Him, just look at Him. Just be occupied with Him. Forget about trying to be like Him. Instead of letting that fill our mind and heart, let Him fill it. Just behold Him, look upon Him through the Word. Come to the Word for one purpose and that is to meet the Lord. Not to get your mind crammed full of things about the sacred Word, but come to it to meet the Lord. Make it to be a medium, not of Biblical scholarship, but of fellowship with Christ. Behold the Lord."

> Thou sayest, "Fit me, fashion me for Thee."
>   Stretch forth thine empty hands, and be thou still:
> O restless soul, thou dost but hinder Me
>   By valiant purpose and by steadfast will.
> Behold the summer flowers beneath the sun,
>   In stillness his great glory they behold;
> And sweetly thus his mighty work is done,
>   And resting in his gladness they unfold.
> So are the sweetness and the joy divine
>   Thine, O beloved, and the work is Mine.
>   —Ter Steegen

"For it is God which worketh in you both to will and to do of his good pleasure" (Phil. 2:13). And what is His "good pleasure" He is performing in us? He is working everything together for this one purpose: "That the life also of Jesus might be made manifest in our mortal flesh" (II Cor. 4:11). This is life: "For to me to live is Christ" (Phil. 1:21). This is service: "And there were certain Greeks . . . saying, Sir, we would see Jesus" (John 12:20,21).

PREPARATION

Once we know His eternal plan and purpose for us, plus His method of preparation and process to that end, there is rest and confidence. Now it so happens that God's basic ingredient for growth is need. Without personal needs, we would get nowhere in our Christian life. The reason our Father creates and allows needs in our lives is to turn us from all that is outside of Christ, centering us in Him alone. "Not I, but Christ" (Gal. 2:20).

For both our growth and our service it is all essential that we see and understand this principle, which J. B. Stoney sets forth in a sentence: "The soul never imbibes the truth in living power but as it requires it." As for our growth, needs cause us to reach out and appropriate by faith, from our Lord Jesus, that which we require. And in the matter of service, in witnessing and helping others, we must watch and wait for the hungry, the needy heart, if there is to be abiding fruit. Again Mr. Stoney says, "The true value of anything is known only when it is wanted." Mr. Darby makes this doubly clear by writing: "Wisdom and philosophy never found out God; He makes Himself known to us through our needs; necessity finds Him out. I doubt much if we have ever learned anything solidly except we have learnt it thus."

In this light, our needs are invaluable! We must face up to the fact that without spiritual hunger, we cannot feed on the Lord Jesus Christ. From our personal experience Matthew 5:6 should mean much to every one of us: "Blessed are they which do hunger and thirst after righteousness: for they shall be filled." All too often believers are exhorted and even pressured to grow before there is an acute awareness of need, before there is true spiritual hunger. And, sad to say, in most instances when there is real heart hunger, very little spiritual food is offered. One of the main reasons why so much evangelistic effort and personal witnessing comes to little or nothing is that truths are forced on the "victim" to be saved before he is aware that he is lost. The work will soon come to naught unless an overpowering conviction of sin causes the lost to reach out with the grip of personal faith and find their need fully met in the Saviour.

Watchman Nee puts first things first in saying, "God does not set us here first of all to preach or to do any work for Him. The first thing for which He sets us here is to create in others a hunger for Himself.... No true work will ever begin in a life without first of all a sense of need being created.... We cannot inject spiritual appetite by force into others; we cannot compel people to be hungry. Hunger has to be created, and it can be created in others only by those who carry with them the impressions of God."

In preparation, there is a tearing down before there can be a building up. "Come, and let us return unto the Lord: for he hath torn, and he will heal us; he hath smitten, and he will bind us up" (Hos. 6:1). This applies to both growth and service. J. C. Metcalfe faithfully writes: "It is more than comforting to realize that it is those who have plumbed the depths of failure to whom God invariably gives the call to shepherd others. This is not a call given to the gifted, the highly trained, or the polished as such.

"Without a bitter experience of their own inadequacy and poverty they are quite unfitted to bear the burden of spiritual ministry. It takes a man who has discovered something of the measures of his own weakness to be patient with the foibles of others. Such a man also has a first-hand knowledge of the loving care of the Chief Shepherd, and His ability to heal one who has come humbly to trust in Him and Him alone. Therefore he does not easily despair of others, but looks beyond sinfulness, willfulness, and stupidity, to the might of unchanging love. The Lord Jesus does not give the charge, 'Be a shepherd to My lambs . . . to My sheep,' on hearing Peter's self-confident affirmation of undying loyalty, but He gives it after he has utterly failed to keep his vows and has wept bitterly in the streets of Jerusalem."

Yes, there is going to be deep, thorough and long preparation if there is to be reality—if our life is to be Christ-centered, our walk controlled by the Holy Spirit and our service glorifying to God. Sooner or later the Holy Spirit begins to make us aware of our basic problem as believers—the infinite difference between self and Christ. "There are other laborers besides those who are seeking for pardon—for justification. There are laborers for sanctification—after personal holiness—after riddance of the power of the old Adam; and to such, as well as to those who are seeking after salvation, Christ promises, with this great 'I will' (Matt. 11:28-30). It is highly possible for a man, after having found justifying rest in Christ, to enter upon a state of deep need as regards sanctifying rest. We think we shall not go far wrong if we say that this has been the experience of almost every believer that has ever lived" (P. B. Power).

Much of His preparation in our lives consists of

setting up this struggle—our seeing self for what it is and then attempting to get free from its evil power and influence. For there is no hope of consistent abiding in the Lord Jesus as long as we are under the dominion of the self-life, in which "dwelleth no good thing" (Rom. 7:18). "Not in babyhood are we able to continually abide in His presence, regardless of our surroundings and that which we are doing. Not when we serve Him with intermittent zeal does our own soul grow and thrive; not when we are indifferent are we watered from the presence of the Lord. It is after we have been subdued, refined, and chastened; when love of self and the world is gone, that we learn to abide in touch with Him at all times, and in all places or surroundings" (MacIlravy).

The value of both the struggle to free ourselves from the old Adam-life and the equally fruitless efforts to experience the new Adam-life, the Christ-life, is to finally realize that it is utterly futile. Our personal, heart-breaking failure in every phase of our Christian life is our Father's preparation for His success on our behalf. This negative processing of His finally brings us into His positive promise of Philippians 1:6: "Being confident of this very thing, that he which hath begun a good work in you will perform it until the day of Jesus Christ." His "good work" in us is begun through failure (and this includes our strongest points), which continues on into His success by His performance and not ours. "For it is God which worketh in you both to will and to do of his good pleasure" (2:13). There is no question but that we all began in sheer grace, and we must continue and arrive on the very same basis: "Stand fast therefore in the liberty wherewith Christ hath made us free" (Gal. 5:1).

Charles Trumbull said, "The effortless life is not the will-less life. We use our will to believe, to receive, but not to exert effort in trying to accomplish what only God can do. Our hope for victory over sin is not 'Christ plus my efforts,' but 'Christ plus my receiving.' To receive victory from Him is to believe His Word that solely by His grace He is, this moment, freeing us from the dominion of sin. And to believe on Him in this way is to recognize that He is doing for us what we cannot do for ourselves." We learned this principle at the time of our spiritual birth, and it seems that most of us have to learn it all over again for our spiritual growth and service. Fear not, dear friend; just hold firm to the fact of His purpose for you in Christ, and He will faithfully take you step by step into all the necessary preparation—He will do it. Once you are sure of the purpose, you can be equally positive of the preparation. Simply remember that Romans 8:28 and 29 go together, and thank Him for Philippians 1:6.

"The Lord is glorified in a people whose heart is set at any cost, by any road, upon the goal which is God Himself. A man who is thus minded says, 'By any road!' Here is a very difficult road, a road beset by enemies, but the passionate desire for the goal will hold him steadfast in the way. It is the man who lacks the yearning to know Him that will easily be turned aside. Along that road the Man Christ Jesus has already gone before, and at every point has overcome for us. We have not to climb up; we are to be brought through in the train of His triumph. Every enemy has been met; every foe has been overcome; there remains nothing that has not been put potentially beneath His feet, and there remains nothing in this universe that is able to overcome the least child of God who has taken the hand of the Lord and said: 'Lord, bring me through to the place where Thou art, in virtue of the blood which Thou hast already taken through in victory.' There is great glory to the Lord in a quiet, confident walk in a day of adversity, a day of dread, when things about us are shaking and trembling" (G. P.).

COMPLETE IN HIM

We continue to deal with foundational facts, since the life can be no better than its root, its source. Youth and immaturity tend to act first and think later, if at all. Maturity has learned to take time to assess the facts. Our patient Husbandman is willing for us to take time and learn the eternal facts, without which we cannot be brought to maturity.

Our Lord Jesus so often uses natural facts in order to teach the deepest spiritual truths. He first teaches us about our natural, Adamic life before we can understand and appreciate our new spiritual Christ-life. This involves the vital source principle—"after his image" (Gen. 5:3). Every believer first learns that he is complete in Adam—he sprang from him; he is like him. "For as by one man's disobedience many were made sinners" (Rom. 5:19). "For I know that in me (that is, in my flesh) dwelleth no good thing" (7:18). When, through our failures and struggles, He has taught us about the natural, we will be ready to learn of our spiritual Source. "By the obedience of one shall many be made righteous" (5:19). "For in him dwelleth all the fulness of the Godhead bodily. And ye are complete in him" (Col. 2:9,10).

There are two main aspects to this source principle. First, the Lord Jesus is the source of our Christian life—we were born into Him; God has made us complete in Him. This truth we are to hold by faith; it is true of each of us. "If any man be in Christ, he is a new creature" (II Cor. 5:17). Second, as we hold to this fact by faith, we are brought into the practical reality of it day by day in our experience. Little by little we receive that which is already ours. The important thing to know and be sure of is that all is ours; we are complete in Him—*now*. This fact enables us to hold still while He patiently works into our character that life of ours which is hid with Christ in God.

"Progress is only advancing in the knowledge, the spiritual knowledge, of what we really possess at the outset. It is like ascending a ladder. The ladder is grace. The first step is, we believe that the Lord Jesus was sent of God; second, that in the fulness of His work we are justified; third, we make His acquaintance; fourth, we come to see Him in heaven; we know our association with Him there, and His power here; fifth, we learn the mystery, the great things we are entitled to because of being His body; sixth, that we are seated in heavenly places in Christ; seventh, lost in wonder and in praise in the knowledge of Himself" (J. B. Stoney).

Since we are complete in our Lord Jesus, it will not do to try and add to that finished work. It is now a matter of walking by faith and receiving, or appropriating from the ever-abundant source within. Walter Marshall is concise here: "Christ's resurrection was our resurrection to a life of holiness, as Adam's fall was our fall into spiritual death. And we are not ourselves the first makers and formers of our new holy nature, any more than of our original corruption, but both are formed ready for us to partake of them. And by union with Christ, we partake of that spiritual life that He took possession of for us at His resurrection, and thereby we are enabled to bring forth the fruits of it; as the Scripture showeth by the similitude of a marriage union. Romans 7:4: 'Married to another, even to him who is raised from the dead, that we should bring forth fruit unto God.' "

Our part is not production but reception of our life in Christ. This entails Bible-based fact-finding, explicit faith in Him and His purpose for us in Christ and patient trust while He takes us through the necessary processing involved. No believer ever fell into maturity, even though he is complete in Christ. Spiritual growth necessitates heart-hunger for the Lord Jesus, determination, based on assurance, to have that which is ours in Him, plus meditation and thought. We will never come into the knowledge of our spiritual possessions through a superficial understanding of the Word. How can we ever expect to have intimate fellowship with One we know little of?

The following truth by J. T. Beck may be a good opportunity to exercise and develop some of that meditation and thought: "What is needed is a mediation, in which God concentrates His own peculiar Spirit and Life as a principle in a human individual to be personally appropriated. In a revelation, which is really to translate the Divine into man's individual personal life, in truth, to form men of God, the Divine as such—that is, as a personal life—must first be embodied in a personal center in humanity. For this reason: as soon as something strictly new is concerned, something that in its peculiarity has not yet existed, every new type of life, before it can multiply itself to a number of specimens, must first have its full contents combined in perfect unity, in an adequate new principle. And so, for the making personal of the Divine among men, the first thing needed is one in whom the principle of the Divine life has become personal.

"Christianity concentrates the whole fulness of revelation in the one human personality of Jesus Christ as Mediator—that is, as the mediating central principle of the new Divine organism, in its fulness of Spirit and Life, in and for the human personal life. With the entrance of Christ into the human individual, the Divine life becomes imminent in us, not in its universal world-relation, but as a personal principle, so that man is not only a being made of God, but a being begotten of God. And with the growing transformation of the individual into the life-type of Christ there is perfected the development of the personal life out of God, in God, and to God—the development not only of a moral or theocratic communion, but a communion of nature!"

A seed embodies in full the reproduction of the life from which it came. That much is complete and can never be added to. "Being born again, not of corruptible seed, but of incorruptible" (I Pet. 1:23). "Thou shalt not sow thy field with mingled seed" (Lev. 19:19). It is to be "not I, but Christ" (Gal. 2:20). The Seed has been implanted—now the entire question is one of growth and maturity. This alone will bring forth fruit that abides. "The development of the divine life in the Christian is like the natural growth in the vegetable world. We do not need to make any special effort, only place ourselves under the conditions favorable to such growth."

Only those who have sought to grow by effort and failed are in the position to appreciate the fact that God is the aggressor in the realm of development. "All the powers of Deity which have already wrought together in the accomplishment of the first part of the eternal purpose, the revealing of the Father's perfect likeness in the Man Christ Jesus, are equally engaged to accomplish the second part, and work that likeness in each of God's children."

William Law agrees: "A root set in the finest soil, in the best climate, and blessed with all that sun and air and rain can do for it, is not so sure a way of its growth to perfection, as every man may be whose spirit aspires after all that which God is ready and infinitely desirous to give him. For the sun meets not the springing bud that stretches toward him with half that certainty as God, the Source of all good, communicates Himself to the soul that longs to partake of Him."

Not only is our life complete in Him but likewise the essential victory in all the many exigencies of that life. "When you fight to get victory, then you have lost the battle at the very outset. Suppose the Enemy assaults you in your home or in your business. He creates a situation with which you cannot possibly deal. What do you do? Your first instinct is to prepare yourself for a big battle and then pray to God to give you the victory in it. But if you do so defeat is sure, for you have given up the ground that is yours in Christ. By the attitude you have taken you have relinquished it to the Enemy. What then should you do when he attacks? You should simply look up and praise the Lord. 'Lord, I am faced with a situation that I cannot possibly meet. Thine enemy the Devil has brought it about to compass my downfall, but I praise Thee that Thy victory is an all-inclusive victory. It covers this situation, too. I praise Thee that I have already full victory in this matter' " (Watchman Nee).

Don't rush—He won't. "The Japanese artist,

Hokusai, said, 'From the age of six I had a mania for drawing the forms of things. By the time I was fifty I had published an infinity of designs; but nothing I produced before seventy is worth considering.' He died at eighty-nine, declaring that if he could have only another five years he would have become a great artist."

APPROPRIATION

Here is an important subject that has to do with faith and the practical reception of that which we are able to trust Him for. Appropriation does not necessarily mean to gain something new but to set aside for our practical possession something that already belongs to us.

In order to appropriate something for our daily walk in Christ, there are two essentials: to see what is already ours in Christ; and to be aware of our need for it. On these two factors rests the ability to appropriate—to reach out in steadfast faith and receive that which belongs to us in our Lord Jesus Christ.

Regarding the first essential, to *see* that which is already ours, William R. Newell wrote: "Paul does not ask a thing of the saints in the first three chapters of Ephesians but just to listen while he proclaims that wondrous series of great and eternal FACTS concerning them; and not until he has completed this catalogue of realities about them does he ask them to do anything at all!

"And when he does open his plea for their high walk as saints, everything is based on the revelation before given the facts of their high character and destiny as saints: 'I therefore ... beseech you that ye walk worthy of the vocation wherewith ye are called' (Eph. 4:1). Let us cease laying down to the saints long lists of 'conditions' of entering into the blessed life in Christ; and instead, as the primal preparation for leading them into the experience of this life, show them what their position, possessions, and privileges in Christ already are. Thus shall we truly work with the Holy Spirit, and thus shall we have more, and much more abiding fruit of our labors among the people of God."

Once we see that which is ours in Christ Jesus, practical need will cause us to appropriate, to receive, the answer to that need. "There was a 'supply of the Spirit of Jesus Christ' for Paul, and that made it possible for Christ to be magnified in him. It was a supply which was always available, but only appreciated and appropriated as and when the Apostle came to know his need. Life is meant to bring a succession of discoveries of our need of Christ, and with every such discovery the way is opened for a new inflow of the supply. This is the explanation of so much that we cannot otherwise understand—this plunging of us into new tests where only a fresh supply of the Spirit of Jesus Christ will meet our need. And as our need is met, as we prove the sufficiency of Christ to meet our inward need, so there can be a new showing forth of His glory through us" (H. F).

These two realities of seeing and needing bring us from childish meandering into a responsible, specific walk of faith. They take us from the "help me" attitude to that of giving thanks; from begging to appropriation. Notice what L. L. Letgers, co-founder of Wycliffe Bible Translators, has to say about this, referring to Ephesians 1:3: "Blessed be the God and Father of our Lord Jesus Christ, who hath blessed us with all spiritual blessings in the heavenly places in Christ": "If you run over in your mind and find one single blessing with which God might bless us today, with which He has not already blessed us, then what He told Paul was not true at all, because he said, 'God hath.' It is all done. 'It is finished.' God hath blessed us with every spiritual blessing in the heavenlies! The great pity of it all is that we are saying, 'O God bless us, bless us in this, bless us in that!' and it is all done. He has blessed us with every spiritual blessing in the heavenlies." As C. A. Coates said, "It is appropriation that tests us. How often we stop at admiration."

From time to time the Holy Spirit will bring to our attention a certain aspect of the Word in a striking manner, and we will rejoice to see and believe that it is ours in Christ. It may be, for instance, the truths of Matthew 11:28: "Come unto me, all ye that labour and are heavy laden, and I will give you rest." Besides the usual personal situations, the uncertainty, strife and tensions of world conditions provide just what is needed for the believer to abide, to rest, in the Lord Jesus. The need exists, and when he sees the rest in Him, all there remains to do is to appropriate!

So far so good. The believer sees what he possesses in Christ, and the need enables him to reach out and confidently appropriate and accept the required rest. This appropriation must be a case of clear, scriptural, specific trust. We are not to "ask amiss." And now comes the critical phase, the key to it all. In most instances of appropriation there is a waiting period between the acceptance and the receiving—often of years. Our responsibility is to patiently wait on Him during the time necessary for Him to work into our character, our life, that which we have appropriated in Christ—in this instance, His rest, steadiness, assurance and security. Isaiah 64:4 refers to what God "hath prepared for [does in behalf of] him that waiteth for him."

T. Austin-Sparks gives us two valuable thoughts regarding this all-important gap—usually a matter of years—between the actual appropriation and the practical experience. "Every bit of truth we receive, if we receive it livingly, will take us into conflict and will be established through conflict. It will be worthless until there has been a battle over it. Take any position the Lord calls you to take, and, if you are taking it with Him, you are going through things in it, and there will be an element added by reason of the battle. You have taken a position—yes, but you have not really got it yet, the real value of it has not been proved. You have not come into the real significance of it until there has been some sore conflict in relation to it. . . .

"As the result of the work of His cross, and as the grand issue of His resurrection, eternal life is received already by those who believe. But while that life is itself victorious, incorruptible, indestructible, the believer has to come by faith to prove it, to live by it, to learn its laws, to be conformed to it. There is a deposit in the believer, which in itself needs no addition, so far as its quality is concerned. So far as its victory, its power, its glory, its potentialities are concerned nothing can be added to it. But the course of spiritual experience, of spiritual life, is to discover, to appropriate, and to live by all that the life represents and means."

Now we have seen a third element involved in our appropriation. After we have seen our possessions in Christ and become aware of our need, then we must give Him the necessary time to work the appropria-

tion into our everyday walk. If we are looking for our
needs to be met in the next interview, the next devotional book, the next series of special meetings, the
next hoped for "revival," then reality will never
come.

In this matter of Christian development there is no
shortcut, no quick and easy way. The Husbandman
builds into the believer that which He intends to
minister through him to others. In order to minister
Life to others, what one does and says must flow
from what he is. "For it pleased the Father that in
him [Christ Jesus] should all fulness dwell" (Col.
1:19); "For we are made partakers of Christ" (Heb.
3:14); "That ye might be filled with all the fulness of
God" (Eph. 3:19); "Your life is hid with Christ in
God" (Col. 3:3); "That the life also of Jesus might be
made manifest in our mortal flesh" (II Cor. 4:11).

How often we simply admire and talk about truths
the Holy Spirit reveals to us in the Word, whereas
His primary purpose in giving them to us is that we
might stand on them in faith, waiting confidently
for Him to make them an integral part of our life. "A
prophet is one who has a history, one who has been
dealt with by God, one who has experienced the for-
mative work of the Spirit. We are sometimes asked
by would-be preachers how many days should be
spent in preparation of a sermon. The answer is: At
least ten years, and probably nearer twenty! For the
preacher matters to God at least as much as the
thing preached. God chooses as His prophets those
in whom He has already worked what He intends to
use as His message for today" (Watchman Nee).

IDENTIFICATION

As our thinking moves along from the substitutionary (birth) truths on to the identification (growth) truths, it might be good to consider briefly what leaders, honored of God through the years, have to say about identification, as centered in Romans 6.

Evan H. Hopkins: "The trouble of the believer who knows Christ as his justification is not sin as to its guilt, but sin as to its ruling power. In other words, it is not from sin as a load, or an offence, that he seeks to be freed—for he sees that God has completely acquitted him from the charge and penalty of sin—but it is from sin as a master. To know God's way of deliverance from sin as a master he must apprehend the truth contained in the sixth chapter of Romans. There we see what God has done, not with our sins—that question the Apostle dealt with in the preceding chapters—but with ourselves, the agents and slaves of sin. He has put our old man—our original self—where He put our sins, namely, on the cross with Christ. 'Knowing this, that our old man was crucified with him' (Rom. 6:6). The believer there sees not only that Christ died for him—substitution—but that he died with Christ—identification" (*Thoughts on Life and Godliness*, p. 50).

Andrew Murray: "Like Christ, the believer too has died to sin; he is one with Christ, in the likeness of His death (Rom. 6:5). And as the knowledge that

Christ died for sin as our atonement is indispensable to our justification; so the knowledge that Christ and we with Him in the likeness of His death, are dead to sin, is indispensable to our sanctification" (*Like Christ*, p. 176).

J. Hudson Taylor: "Since Christ has thus dwelt in my heart by faith, how happy I have been! I am dead and buried with Christ—ay, and risen too! And now Christ lives in me, and 'the life which I now live in the flesh I live by the faith of the Son of God, who loved me, and gave himself for me' [Gal. 2:20]. Nor should we look upon this experience, these truths, as for the few. They are the birthright of every child of God, and no one can dispense with them without dishonoring our Lord" (*Spiritual Secret*, p. 116).

William R. Newell: "To those who refuse or neglect to reckon themselves dead to sin as God commands, we press the question, How are you able to believe that Christ really bare the guilt of your sins and that you will not meet them at the judgment day? It is only *God's Word* that tells you Christ bare your sins in His own body on the tree. And it is *that same Word* that tells you that you, as connected with Adam, died with Christ, that your old man was crucified, that since you are in Christ you shared His death unto sin, and are thus to reckon your present relation to sin in Christ—as one who is dead to it, and alive unto God" (*Romans, Verse by Verse*, p. 227).

Lewis Sperry Chafer: "The theme under consideration is concerned with the death of Christ as that death is related to the divine judgments of the sin nature in the child of God. The necessity for such judgments and the sublime revelation that these judgments are now fully accomplished for us is unfolded in Romans 6:1-10. This passage is the foundation as well as the key to the possibility of a 'walk in the Spirit' " (*He That Is Spiritual*, p. 154).

Ruth Paxson: "The old 'I' in you and me was judicially crucified with Christ. 'Ye died' and your death dates from the death of Christ. 'The old man,' the old 'Self' in God's reckoning was taken to the Cross with Christ and crucified and taken into the tomb with Christ and buried.... Assurance of deliverance from the sphere of the 'flesh' and of the dethronement of 'the old man' rests upon the apprehension and acceptance of this fact of co-crucifixion" (*Life on the Highest Plane*, Vol. II, pp. 78,79).

Watchman Nee: "The Blood can wash away my sins, but it cannot wash away my 'old man.' It needs the cross to crucify me ... the sinner.... Our sins are dealt with by the Blood, but we ourselves are dealt with by the Cross. The Blood procures our pardon; ... the Cross procures our deliverance from what we are" (*The Normal Christian Life*, pp. 31,32).

L. E. Maxwell: "Believers in Christ were joined to Him at the cross, united to Him in death and resurrection. We died with Christ. He died for us, and we died with Him. This is a great fact, true of all believers" (*Christian Victory*, p. 11).

Norman B. Harrison: "This is the distinctive mark of the Christian—the experience of the cross. Not merely that Christ died for us, but that we died with Him. 'Knowing this, that our old man is crucified with him' (Rom. 6:6)" (*His Side Versus Our Side*, p. 40).

F. J. Huegel: "If the great Luther, with his stirring message of justification by faith, had with Paul moved on from Romans 5 to Romans 6 with its amazing declarations concerning the now justified sinner's position of identification with his crucified Lord, would not a stifled Protestantism be on higher ground today? Might it not be free from its ulcerous fleshiness?" (*The Cross of Christ*, p. 84).

Alexander R. Hay: "The believer has been united with Christ in His death. In this union with Christ, the flesh, 'the body of sin'—the entire fallen, sin-ruined being with its intelligence, will and desires—is judged and crucified. By faith, the believer reckons (counts) himself 'dead unto sin' (Rom. 6:3-14)" (*N. T. Order for Church & Missionary*, p. 310).

T. Austin-Sparks: "The first phase of our spiritual experience may be a great and overflowing joy, with a marvelous sense of emancipation. In this phase extravagant things are often said as to total deliverance and final victory. Then there may, and often does, come a phase of which inward conflict is the chief feature. It may be very much of a Romans seven experience. This will lead, under the Lord's hand, to the fuller knowledge of the meaning of identification with Christ, as in Romans six. Happy is the man who has been instructed in this from the beginning" (*What Is Man?* p. 61).

J. Penn-Lewis: "If the difference between 'Christ dying for us,' and 'our dying with Him,' has not been recognized, acknowledged, and applied, it may safely be affirmed that the self is still the dominating factor in the life" (*Memoir*, p. 26).

William Culbertson: "Who died on the cross? Of course, our blessed Lord died on the cross; but who else died there? 'Knowing this, that our old man was crucified with him, that the body of sin might be done away, that we should no longer be in bondage to sin; for he that hath died is justified from sin. But if we died with Christ, we believe that we shall also live with him' (Rom. 6:6-8)" (*God's Provision for Holy Living*, p. 46).

Reginald Wallis: "God says in effect, 'My child, as you reckoned on the substitutionary work of the Lord Jesus Christ for your salvation, now go a step farther and reckon on His representative work for your victory day by day.' You believe the Lord Jesus died for your sins because God said so. Now take the next step. Accept by faith the further fact that you died with Him, i.e., that your 'old man was crucified with Him'" (*The New Life*, p. 51).

James R. McConkey: "Because He died 'death hath no more dominion over Him,' and because of our union with Him 'sin shall not have dominion over you,' even though it is present in you. Our 'reckoning' ourselves dead to sin in Jesus Christ does not make it a fact—it is already a fact through our union with Him. Our reckoning it to be true only makes us begin to realize the fact in experience" (*The Way of Victory*, p. 16).

CONSECRATION

It might be good to stress several points just here. (1) Never was a believer brought into healthy spiritual maturity by means of pressure meetings and constant exhortation nor before he was prepared by the Spirit. (2) Healthy progress is based on the apprehension, understanding and appropriation of the truths in Christ that make for real growth. (3) The experiential aspect of all truth, and especially these so-called deeper truths, is closed to all but the needy heart. Until one is aware of his need to progress spiritually, he will never be brought beyond the birth truths—a mere babe in Christ. "Therefore let us go on and get past the elementary stage in the teachings and doctrine of Christ, the Messiah, advancing steadily toward the completeness and perfection that belongs to spiritual maturity. Let us not again be laying the foundation of repentance and abandonment of dead works [dead formalism], and of the faith [by which you turned] to God" (Heb. 6:1, Amplified).

This subject of consecration seems to be badly misunderstood by so many believers. Many, especially those who are young in the Lord, have been victimized time and time again in this matter of surrender, or commitment. The bludgeon most commonly used is: "The Lord Jesus gave His all for you, now the least you can do is give your all for Him!" The believer is exhorted and pressured to consecrate, surrender, commit his life to Christ on the basis of his love and gratitude for what has been done on his behalf at Calvary.

How often the average congregation is put through this routine. How often the individual believer is maneuvered down front to consecrate and reconsecrate, surrender and resurrender, commit and recommit himself to Christ! Why is it that after a while the believer comes to dread such meetings and messages? Well, there are a number of reasons for all this frustration, floundering and failure; and, praise the Lord, there are scriptural answers available to all who need and want them.

First of all, it is utterly futile to expect a believer, by means of consecration, surrender or commitment, to step from his ground of substitution as spoken of in Romans 3—5 on to that of the deeper truths in Romans 8 and 12:1.

There is the all-important area of identification truth in Romans 6,7 that cannot be skipped over. Every hungry-hearted Christian yearns to be fully consecrated and conditioned for an effective life and service. And from the very outset, until hard experience teaches him otherwise, the well-meaning believer thinks that since he has the will to obey God and to be what He intends for him, he should attempt to carry it out through personal consecrated effort with His help. He seeks to struggle forward via the love motive; i.e., He did for me, so I must do for Him.

The following two thoughts by Andrew Murray will help here. "A superficial acquaintance with God's plan leads to the view that while justification is God's work, by faith in Christ, sanctification (growth) is our work, to be performed under the influence of the gratitude we feel for the deliverance we have experienced, and by the aid of the Holy Spirit. But the earnest Christian soon finds how little gratitude can supply the power. When he thinks that more prayer will supply it, he finds that, indispensable as prayer is, it is not enough. Often the believer struggles hopelessly for years, until he listens to the teaching of the Spirit, as He glorifies Christ again, and reveals Christ, our Sanctification, to be appropriated by faith alone. . . .

"God works to will, and He is ready to work to do (Phil. 2:13), but, alas! many Christians misunderstand this. They think because they have the will it is enough, and that now they are able to do. This is not so. The new will is a permanent gift, an attribute of the new nature. The power to do is not a permanent gift, but must be each moment received from the Holy Spirit. It is the man who is conscious of his own impotence as a believer who will learn that by the Holy Spirit he can lead a holy life." Now and then one is called on to speak out against something that is good in order to present His best. The love motive from which to live the Christian life and serve the Lord is good; it is high, but it is not adequate— especially because it is not the motivation underwritten by Him.

As growing Christians, it is time for us to see the necessity of going beyond the love motive to the life motive. "For to me to live is Christ" (Phil. 1:21). Our consecration, surrender or commitment will never hold up if it is our responding to Him from any other motivation than the response of His life in us. Yielding to Him on any different basis will simply amount to our trying to live for Him in the self-life. And even if that were possible, He could never accept it, since in that realm there dwells no good thing (Rom. 7:18), plus the fact that He has already taken the old life to the cross and crucified it (see Rom. 6:6; Gal. 2:20; II Tim. 2:11; I Pet. 2:24).

J. C. Metcalfe sees both the problem and the answer: "The modern teaching of consecration, which is tantamount to the consecration of the 'old man,' seeks to bypass the death sentence and, therefore, only leads to frustration and failure. When, however, you and I are prepared, in simple humility, to make the *fact* of our death with Christ our daily basis of life and service, there is nothing that can prevent the uprising and outflow of new life, and meet the need of thirsty souls around us."

Here is the crux of the matter. The question is: Which life is to be consecrated to Him—the old self-life, or the new Christ-life? God can accept absolutely nothing from the old—He sees and acknowledges only that which is centered in His Son, who is our life. Hence God has but one stipulation for consecration: "Yield yourselves unto God, as those that are alive from the dead" (Rom. 6:13). This is our only ground, and from this platform we are to count ourselves dead to sin, self, the law and the world and alive to God in the risen Christ—to walk in "newness of life" (Rom. 6:4), "risen life" (see v. 11).

"Yield [present] yourselves unto God, as . . . alive from the dead" (Rom. 6:13). "This is the true place of consecration. For believers to 'consecrate themselves to God' ere they have learnt their union with Christ in death and resurrection (identification) is only to present to God the members of the natural man, which He cannot accept. Only those 'alive from the dead'—that is, having appropriated fully their likeness with Him in death—are bidden to present their members as instruments unto God" (J. Penn-Lewis).

"God asks us to present our bodies as living sacrifices to Him (Rom. 12:1). Until we have done this, there is nothing else we can do. Notice this exhortation comes after Romans six. There is a reason for this order—crucifixion comes before consecration. Uncrucified self refuses to be consecrated. This is why so many people with all sincerity walk down the aisles again and again, consecrating uncrucified self to God" (H. Duncan).

This is why the identification truths must be carefully and thoroughly presented, ultimately understood and their reality entered into. We cannot even get as far as consecration without them! Many feel that identification is an "emphasis," an interesting subject ministered at a few Deeper Life Conferences and Keswick Conventions. But these truths are not peripheral, they are foundational. "The sixth of Romans is not an aspect of the truth, but the foundation truth upon which every believer must stand to know anything about victory" (DeV. Fromke). "All the (identification) truths we have learned about the cross, of our death with Christ, our death to sin with Him, of our conformity to death like the grain of wheat falling into the ground to die, are preparatory to the overcoming life. They are the foundation of, and fundamental to it" (J. Penn-Lewis).

"A careful study of all the Epistles of Paul will show that they are written on the basis of the cross set forth in Romans six—the fact that God consigns the old fallen Adam-life to the cross, and has nothing to say to it. God deals with all believers on the ground—'In Christ you died.' But the Church of Christ, as a whole, ignores this fact. It treats the fallen creation (self-life) as capable of improvement, and the meaning of the cross bringing to death the old Adam race as fallen beyond repair, is thus nullified" (DeV. Fromke).

SELF

One of the most important factors in Christian growth is the Holy Spirit's revelation of the self-life to the believer. Self is the fleshly, carnal life of nature, the life of the first Adam—"dead in trespasses and sins" (Eph. 2:1); thoroughly corrupt before God (see Gal. 5:19-21); the life in which there is no good thing in the sight of God (Rom. 7:18). Nowhere do spiritual principles mean more than here. Plato, with his "Know thyself," was more right than he knew but still only half right. Paul, with God's "Not I, but Christ" (Gal. 2:20), was all right!

In order for one to get beyond just knowing about the Lord Jesus and enter into a consistent and growing personal knowledge of, and fellowship with, Him, one must *first* come to know oneself. Introspection is not involved here—the Holy Spirit uses experiential revelation. First, the believer learns "Not I"; then, "but Christ." First, "Except a corn of wheat fall into the ground and die, it abideth alone"; then, "but if it die, it bringeth forth much fruit" (John 12:24). First, "alway delivered unto death"; then, "that the life also of Jesus might be made manifest" (II Cor. 4:11). In service it is first, "death worketh in us"; then, "but life in you" (v. 12). All resurrection life springs out of death or else it would not be resurrection life—His risen life (see Rom. 6:5,6). We are to yield ourselves to God as those that are alive from the dead (v. 13).

For some years now the scene has been dominated by a conversion known as "commitment," which often, sad to say, amounts to little more than a spiritual miscarriage. When there is a bit of life, it usually blossoms overnight into full bloom and soon becomes heavy with the fruit of "dynamic," "radiant" personality coupled with busy, rushing service. The tragedy of this sort of thing is that self is at home and thrives in the glow of it all and is rarely found out for what it really is. All is indiscriminate "hearts and flowers."

The healthy new birth, based on deep conviction of sin and repentance toward God, starts out clear and strong with love and devotion to the Saviour. But before long there comes the sickening realization of an element within that pulls one back to self-centeredness, to the world, to the rule of the Law, to sin. This learning by heartbreaking experience of the utter sinfulness and reigning power of self in the everyday Christian life is the means whereby we come to know the Lord Jesus beyond the birth phase—as our Saviour; on to the growth phase—as our Lord and Life. "To me to live is Christ" (Phil. 1:21). No believer will truly come to know the Lord Jesus as his life until he knows by experience the deadly self-life deep within for what it is.

At a Spiritual Life Conference many years ago Dr. C. I. Scofield said, "Not everyone, by any means, has had the experience of the seventh of Romans, that agony of conflict, of desire to do what we cannot do, of longing to do the right we find we cannot do. It is a great blessing when a person gets into the seventh of Romans and begins to realize the awful conflict of its struggle and defeat; because the first step toward getting out of the struggle of the seventh chapter and into the victory of the eighth, is to get into the seventh. Of all the needy classes of people, the neediest of this earth are not those who are having a heart-breaking, agonizing struggle for victory, but those who are having no struggle at all, and no victory, and who do not know it, and who are satisfied and jogging along in a pitiable absence of almost all the possessions that belong to them in Christ."

J. C. Metcalfe gives this same fact an added witness: "Many a young Christian, who has not been warned of this necessary voyage of discovery upon which the Holy Spirit will certainly embark him (Rom. 7), has been plunged into almost incurable despair at the sight of the sinfulness which is his by nature. He has in the first place rejoiced greatly in the forgiveness of his sins, and his acceptance by God; but sooner or later he begins to realize that all is not well, and that he has failed and fallen from the high standard which he set himself to reach in the first flush of his conversion.

"He begins to know something of the experience which Paul so graphically describes: 'What I would, that do I not; but what I hate, that do I' (Rom. 7:15), and, in consequence, he feels that the bottom has fallen out of his Christian life; and then perhaps the Devil whispers to him that it is just no good his going on, because he will never be able to make the grade. Little does he know how healthy his condition is, and that this shattering discovery is but the prelude to a magnificent series of further discoveries of things which God has expressly designed for his eternal enrichment. All through life God has to show us our own utter sinfulness and need, before He is able to lead us on into realms of grace, in which we shall glimpse His glory."

Self-revelation precedes divine revelation—that is a principle for both spiritual birth and spiritual growth. The believer who is going through struggle and failure is the Christian who is being carefully and lovingly handled by his Lord in a very personal way. He is being taken through the experience (years in extent) of self-revelation and into death, the only basis on which to "know him, and the power of his resurrection, and the fellowship of his sufferings, being made conformable unto his death" (Phil. 3:10).

God works by paradox. Success comes via failure; life springs out of death and so on. The only element in the believer's life that crumbles is that which has to go anyway—the new life can never be harmed or affected. This disintegration is something the believer cannot enter into nor engineer on his own—self will never cast out self. He has to be led into it by the mercy of the Holy Spirit—into failure, abject and total. "For we which live are alway delivered unto death for Jesus' sake, that the life also of Jesus might be made manifest in our mortal flesh" (II Cor. 4:11). So often the means utilized by the Spirit is an unsaved mate, or even a saved one! Or poor health; yes, and good health too! A thousand and one things are used by Him—in fact, everything (Rom. 8:28,29), to bring out the worst in us, ultimately enabling us to see that the Christian life has to be "not I, but Christ" (Gal. 2:20). People, circumstances, etc., are never the cause of failure. Self's reaction to them is the cause and the one problem to be dealt with.

"Many of us have probably known what it was to rejoice in the grace of God without having apprehended very much the true character of the flesh. It has often been noticed that where there is the greatest exuberance of joy in young converts, there is often a levity which fails to take into account that the flesh is unchanged. In such cases the grace of God is taken up in a self-confident way; there is very little self-distrust, or sense of weakness and dependence. And the inevitable consequence is a fall, or a succession of falls, that gradually brings home to the consciences of believers their utter weakness and incapacity as in the flesh" (C. A. Coates).

Evan Hopkins shares some important light on our subject: "How infinite are the forms in which self appears. Some are occupied with good self. They pride themselves on their excellencies. Others are just as much occupied with bad self. They are forever groaning over their imperfections, and struggling with the flesh as if they hoped in time to improve it. When shall we be convinced it is so utterly bad that it is beyond all recovery? Our experience, upward, in the power of God, is just in proportion to our experience, downward, in ceasing from self.

"Is it, Reckon yourself to be weak in reference to sin? No, it is lower than that. Is it, Reckon yourself to be dying? No, lower still. 'Reckon yourself to be dead—(Rom. 6:11)—indeed unto sin.' Some believe they are very weak. But what does that imply? That they have some strength. But when a man is dead he has no strength. We must act on the fact that we are dead in reference to sin. We shall not then speak of difficulty as to resisting temptation in reference to ourselves. We shall take the lowest place, and say it is impossible. But we shall know that what is impossible with self is possible with God. We shall take our place on the resurrection side of the cross, and in so doing we leave behind the old self-life for the new

Christ-life. To live in Him who is our Life, is to be in the power of God."

Someone has rightly said, "There are many 'separated from the world' Christians who are not 'separated from themselves' Christians."

SELF-DENIAL

When a believer begins to discover something of the awful tyranny of the self-life or has been endlessly struggling against that tyranny, he becomes intensely concerned about the denial of self with the resultant freedom to rest and grow in Christ. Man has many ways of seeking to escape the thralldom of self; God has but one way. First, then, some of these man-centered methods.

Mortification

Denying oneself certain things for a time, or even for all time, is not even close to the answer since the old nature will adjust and thrive under any conditions—anything short of death to self. "There have been those who have thought that to get themselves out of the way it was necessary to withdraw from society; so they denied all natural human relationships and went into the desert or the mountain or the hermit's cell to fast and labor and struggle to mortify the flesh. While their motive was good it is impossible to commend their method. For it is not scriptural to believe that the old Adam nature can be conquered in that manner. It yields to nothing less than the death of the cross. It is altogether too tough to be killed by abusing the body or starving the affections" (A. W. Tozer).

Conquest

Probably the most drawn out and exhausting effort of all is the believer's struggle to conquer and control this rebel self. More meetings, more Bible study, more prayer are all resorted to, but neither are these God's answer to this problem.

Training

Here is a favorite that has been tried and found wanting down through the ages. Good Christian training and culture in the right homes, churches and schools have been relied on to subdue the old nature and bring it into line.

Revivalism

Another failure has been the practice of holding special meetings once or twice a year. This involves outside leadership (a stranger to the individual problems) and the devastating revival routine (confession, new resolutions, etc.), in the hope that something will change—but it rarely does, and then not for long.

Growth

So many dear Christians just keep plodding (or racing) through the deadening routine of their multitudinous church activities and duties, expecting that in time self will change for the better as they grow. But self never changes into anything but more of the same! "That which is born of the flesh is flesh" (John 3:6). "Sometimes this self is entirely bad, as when it is angry, spiteful, unkind, unjust, untruthful, unloving, catty. In other cases a good exterior conceals an evil heart, as when we are proud of our humility, conceited about our Christian service, boastful of our orthodoxy. And an overforwardness and obvious conceit at the sound of one's own voice spoils many a prayer meeting."

Cleansing

Up-to-the-moment confession and consequent cleansing have also constituted a popular method. However, I John 1:9 has to do with sins already committed and not with the source (self) from which they emanate. "The Blood can wash away my sins, but it cannot wash away my 'old man.' It needs the cross to crucify me . . . the sinner. . . . Our sins are dealt with by the Blood, but we ourselves are dealt with by the Cross. The Blood procures our pardon; . . . the Cross procures our deliverance from what we are" (Watchman Nee).

Experiences

Today one of the prevalent attempts for something better is to go in for "the baptism of the Spirit," speaking in tongues, and so on. This is by far the most dangerous and pathetic trap of all, as it is simply self, neurotically and religiously rampant. "Calvary precedes Pentecost. Death with Christ precedes the fulness of the Spirit. Power! Yes, God's children need power, but God does not give power to the old creation, nor to the uncrucified soul. Satan will give power to the 'old Adam,' but not God."

Which of us does not know something of the failure of our ways, well intentioned as they may be? What most do not know is that this very failure is the path to learning, and entering into, God's way. "For my thoughts are not your thoughts, neither are your ways my ways, saith the Lord. For as the heavens are higher than the earth, so are my ways higher than your ways, and my thoughts than your thoughts" (Isa. 55:8,9). Now just what is God's way of self-denial? He has but one way, and it is on the basis of all His other ways: the principle of the finished work. His way for us in everything is the way He has already traveled, conquered and completed in Christ.

The Cross—God's Way

It was on the cross of Calvary that God, in Christ, dealt fully and finally with self, the nature from which all our sins flow. "We know that our old (unrenewed) self was nailed to the cross with Him in order that [our] body, [which is the instrument] of sin, might be made ineffective and inactive for evil, that we might no longer be the slaves of sin" (Rom. 6:6, Amplified). The reason there is no other way for self to be denied is that God has done the work in this way: our identification with Christ Jesus in His death and resurrection! It is done; now it is ours to believe.

"The 'flesh' will only yield to the cross; not to all the resolutions you may make at a conference, not to any self-effort, not to any attempted self-crucifixion; only to co-crucifixion, crucified together with Christ (Gal. 2:20). It is not by putting yourself to death, but by taking, through faith and surrender, your place of union with Christ in His death. That is the blessed barrier of safety between you and all the attractions of the flesh, and that makes the way open to do the will of God" (G. Watt).

The cross of Calvary resulted in the death of the Lord Jesus, both for sin and to sin. In that He died to sin, He died out of the realm of sin, and He arose into the realm of "newness of life" (Rom. 6:4), eternal life. And our identification with Him on Calvary took us into death, down into the tomb, up into newness of life. First, Romans 6:3—"Baptized into his death"; then, Romans 6:4—"Buried with him"; then, Romans 6:5—"For if we have been planted together in the likeness of his death, we shall be also in the likeness of his resurrection." Also, Colossians 3:3: "For ye are dead, and your life is hid with Christ in God"; therefore, Romans 6:11: "Reckon ye also yourselves to be dead indeed unto sin, but alive unto God through Jesus Christ our Lord."

Praise the Lord! It all happened at Calvary: Our sins were paid for, our sinfulness was dealt with, and both by the ultimate—*death.* And we receive the benefits of the work of the cross simply by reckoning on, or believing in, the finished work of the cross. First, through the Word, we find out what God did about our problem. Then, as we become thoroughly convinced of the fact and begin to understand it clearly, we are able to agree to "reckon" it true. And as we exercise faith in God's fact, we begin to receive the benefits of that finished work in experience. Was it not true in the matter of our justification? Yes, and we will likewise find it to be true in the matter of our emancipation from the slavery of the self-life.

"The powerful effect of the cross with God, in heaven, in the blotting out of guilt, and our renewed union with God, is inseparable from the other effect—the breaking down of the authority of sin over man, by the crucifixion of self. Therefore Scripture teaches us that the cross not only works out a disposition or desire to make such a sacrifice, but it really bestows the power to do so, and completes the work. This appears with wonderful clarity in Galatians. In one place the cross is spoken of as the reconciliation for guilt (3:13). But there are three more places where the cross is even more plainly spoken of as the victory over the power of sin; as the power to hold in the place of death the 'I' of the self-life; of the flesh (the outworking of self); and of the world (2:20; 5:24; 6:14). In these passages our union (identification) with Christ, the crucified One, and the conformity to Him resulting from the union, are represented as the result of the power exercised within us and upon us by the cross" (Andrew Murray).

As we learn to stand on the finished work of Calvary, the Holy Spirit will begin to faithfully and effectively apply that finished work of the cross to the self-life, thereby holding it in the place of death—inactive—resulting in the "not I, but Christ" life (Gal. 2:20).

THE CROSS

Studying these truths is hard work. Right? Although spiritual hunger and need are prime requisites for light and understanding, the Holy Spirit does not release the treasures of the Word quickly nor easily. "Deep calleth unto deep" (Ps. 42:7). We have to be prepared, and even then there is much time and digging and praying and meditation and yearning and experiencing involved. True spiritual reality comes in no other way, but, praise the Lord, it does come in this way!

Understanding and appropriating the facts of the cross proves to be one of the most difficult and trying of all phases for the growing believer. Our Lord holds His most vital and best things in store for those who mean business, for those who hunger and thirst for His very best as it is in our Lord Jesus Christ. The believer's understanding of the two aspects of Calvary gives the key to both spiritual growth and life-giving service.

"Calvary is the secret of it all. It is what He did there that counts, and what He did becomes a force in the life of a Christian when it is appropriated by faith. This is the starting point from which all Godly living must take its rise. We shall never know the experience of Christ's victory in our lives until we are prepared to count (reckon) upon His victory at the cross as the secret of our personal victory today.

71

There is no victory for us which was not first His. What we are to experience He purchased, and what He purchased for us we ought to experience. The beginning of the life of holiness is a faith in the crucified Saviour which sees more than His substitutionary work. It is a faith which sees myself identified with Christ in His death and resurrection."

Actually, our Father has trained every one of us for clear-cut, explicit faith in this second aspect of Calvary: our individual identification with the Lord Jesus in His death to sin and rising onto resurrection ground. This training taught us thoroughly in the first realm: believing and appropriating the finished work of His dying for our sins—justification. Now we are asked just as definitely to believe and appropriate the further aspect: "Knowing this, that our old man is crucified with him" (Rom. 6:6); "Likewise reckon ye also yourselves to be dead indeed unto sin, but alive unto God" (v. 11).

Our intelligent faith, standing on the facts of Calvary, gives the Holy Spirit freedom to bring that finished work into our daily lives. We stood on the fact of His dying *for* our sins, and this act of faith allowed the Holy Spirit to give us our freedom from the penalty of sin—justification. Now, once we come to see the fact of the further aspect, we are urged in the Word to stand on the liberating truth of our dying with Christ in His death *to* sin, which allows the Holy Spirit to bring into our lives freedom from the power, the enslavement, of sin—progressive sanctification. And of course when we stand with Him in glory, we will be forever free from the presence of sin—entirely sanctified and glorified.

"As our Substitute He went to the cross alone, without us, to pay the penalty of our sins; as our

Representative, He took us with Him to the cross, and there, in the sight of God, we all died together with Christ. We may be forgiven because He died in our stead; we may be delivered because we died with Him. God's way of deliverance for us, a race of hopeless incurables, is to put us away in the cross of His Son, and then to make a new beginning by re-creating us in union with Him, the Risen, Living One (II Cor. 5:17). It is the Holy Spirit who will make these great facts real and true in our experience as we cooperate with Him; and so the plague of our hearts will be stayed, and we shall be transformed into the likeness of Christ."

"Through the crucifixion of the old man with Christ the believer has been made dead unto sin, he has been completely freed from sin's power, he has been taken beyond sin's grip, the claim of sin upon him has been nullified. This is the flawless provision of God's grace but this accomplished fact can only become an actual reality in the believer's experience as faith lays hold upon it and enables him moment by moment, day by day, though temptation assail him, 'to reckon' it true. As he reckons, the Holy Spirit makes real; as he continues to reckon, the Holy Spirit continues to make real. Sin need have no more power over the believer than he grants it through unbelief. If he is alive unto sin it will be due largely to the fact that he has failed to reckon himself dead unto sin" (Ruth Paxson).

The Reformation brought into focus once again the emphasis upon spiritual birth, without which there can be no beginning. What is lacking amongst believers to this day is the proper emphasis on *growth*—not just to be saved, and heaven by and by. What sort of salvation would we have if our Father simply saved us from the penalty of our sins and then left us on our own to deal with the power of sin in our Christian life and walk? But most believers feel this is about as far as He went and are struggling to get on the best they can, with His help. And this is the Galatian error, so prominent even now throughout born-again circles. We must be brought back to the two basics: freed from the penalty of sin by His finished work; freed from the power of sin by His finished work. "Justified by faith" (Gal. 3:24); "We walk by faith" (II Cor. 5:7); "As ye have therefore received Christ Jesus the Lord, so walk ye in him" (Col. 2:6).

We are not left to deal with the old life ourselves; it has been dealt with by Christ on the cross. This is the fact which must be known, since on that fact is built the New Testament principle and doctrine of holiness. In other words, Calvary is as much the foundation of sanctification as of justification. Both gifts spring from the same work and are two aspects of the same salvation.

Now, as long as the believer does not know this dual aspect of his salvation, the best he can do is seek to handle his sins via confession (I John 1:9)—that is, after the damage has been done! This takes care of the penalty of the product but not the source. Is it not time we allowed the Holy Spirit to get at the source and cut off this stream of sins before they are committed? Is this not infinitely better than the wreckage caused by sin, even though confessed? When believers get sick and tired of spinning year after year in a spiritual squirrel cage—sinning, confessing, but then sinning again—they will be ready for God's answer to the source of sin, which is death to self, brought forth from the completed work of the cross.

"When God's light first shines into our heart our one cry is for forgiveness, for we realize that we have committed sins before Him; but once we have known forgiveness of sins, we make a new discovery—the discovery of sin, and we realize that we have the nature of a sinner. There is an inward inclination to sin. There is a power within that draws us to sin, and when that power breaks out we commit sins. We may seek and receive forgiveness, but then we sin again; and life goes on in a vicious circle—sinning and being forgiven, but then sinning again. We appreciate God's forgiveness, but we want something more than that, we want deliverance. We need forgiveness for what we have done, but we need deliverance from what we are."

Our reckoning on the finished work of our death to sin, in Christ at Calvary, is God's *one* way of deliverance—there is no other way because that is the way He did it. We learned not to add to a finished work in the matter of justification, and now we must learn not to add to the finished work of emancipation. We will be freed when we enter His prepared freedom—there is no other.

"The believer can never overcome the old man even by the power of the new apart from the death of Christ, and therefore the death of Christ unto sin is indispensable, and unless the cross is made the basis upon which he overcomes the old man, he only drops into another form of morality; in other words, he is seeking by self-effort to overcome self, and the struggle is a hopeless one" (C. Usher).

Marcus Rainford refused to stop short of God's ultimate for freedom: "It is not to be a mere passing impression of the mind when we are undisturbed by active temptation; no mere happy frame of spirit when under temporary refreshing from the presence of the Lord; no self-flattering consciousness of a heart exercised in good works; from none of these is the believer to infer his practical mastery over sin, but on the ground that Christ died unto sin, and [he] liveth unto God through Jesus Christ our Lord."

"I must recognize that the enemy within the camp—the flesh, the old nature, self, I, the old Adam, is a usurper. By faith I must reckon him to be in the place that God put him—crucified with Christ. I must realize that now my life is hid with Christ in God; that He is my life" (Ian Thomas).

DISCIPLESHIP

A disciple is one who first maintains the fellowship of the cross, which results in fellowship with his Lord: discipleship. "The atonement of the cross and the fellowship of the cross must be equally preached as the condition of true discipleship." "Christ is the answer, but the cross is needed to clear the way for Him."

In spiritual progress our Lord never pushes. He is our file leader (see Heb. 12:2), and He leads us step by step. We struggle and fail (self-effort), which sets up a yearning for the answer to this depressing failure. In time we see the scriptural facts of deliverance in the cross (identification), and that in turn produces the required hunger to enter into that freedom, freedom for fellowship with the answer—our risen Lord Jesus.

"Nothing can set us apart for God, nothing can make us holy, except as the cross is working in us, because the cross alone can keep the hindrances to holiness in the place of death" (G. Watt). "Back of all successful work for the lost is an inward spiritual impulse; and back of the impulse is the Holy Spirit who reproduces Christ in us; and the brand mark of it all is the cross, the living experience of which must both enter and control the life before we are fit for service" (J. E. Conant).

Nowhere was our Lord Jesus more explicit and firm than when He mentioned discipleship. "And he said to them all, If any man will come after me, let him deny himself, and take up his cross daily, and follow me" (Luke 9:23). "And whosoever doth not bear his cross, and come after me, cannot be my disciple" (14:27). His reason for this is simple: Self cannot and will not follow Him, but taking up one's cross results in death to self and newness of life in Christ Jesus.

A disciple is one who is free from the old and free for the new. In other words, scriptural words: "dead indeed unto sin, but alive unto God" (Rom. 6:11). And for this the Lord Jesus clearly states that each must take up his cross. Here is the ultimatum, so now to the "how."

But first, how not to take up one's cross: "Christians need to understand that bearing the cross does not in the first place refer to the trials which we call crosses, but to the daily giving up of life, of dying to self, which must mark us as much as it did the Lord Jesus, which we need in times of prosperity almost more than adversity, and without which the fulness of the blessing of the cross cannot be disclosed to us" (Andrew Murray).

"May we cease to confuse the words 'a cross' with 'the cross.' Sometimes believers in self-pity bemoan themselves, and say, 'I have taken, or must take up my cross, and follow Jesus.' Would that we would lose sight of our 'cross' in His cross, then His cross becomes our cross; His death, our death; His grave, our grave; His resurrection, our resurrection; His risen life, our newness of life." No, taking up our cross does not mean the stoical bearing of some heavy burden, hardship, illness, distasteful situation or relationship. Enduring anything of this nature is not bearing one's cross. Taking up the cross may or may not involve such things, but such things do not constitute our cross.

The believer's cross is the cross of Calvary, the one on which he was crucified with Christ (see Gal. 2:20). There the eternal emancipation proclamation was signed with the blood of the Lamb and sealed by the Spirit of God. Every believer is thereby freed from all bondage, but not every believer is aware of this liberating truth.

Sad to say, the only believers who are interested in freedom are those who have come to the place of hating instead of hugging their chains. "It is true that the intellect is stumbled by the cross; yet the antagonism to the cross is mainly moral, both in the sinner and in the saint, for its message is only welcomed by those who desire freedom from the bondage of their sins, and who hunger and thirst after the experiential righteousness of God." Yes, the need must be intense, as Norman Douty says: "The Divine way (via the cross) for spiritual emancipation is just as offensive to the child of God as the Divine way for salvation is to the lost."

When the believer begins to really see the cross for what it is—a place of death—he is inclined to hesitate about choosing such fellowship. Our Lord Jesus understands this well, but there is no other way, since that is the manner in which He finished the work on our behalf. So He simply allows our needs to continue their relentless pressure until we finally bend to His inevitable way of the cross.

We will be ready to take up our cross when self becomes intolerable to us, when we begin to "hate our life" as spoken of in Luke 14:26. This deep burden of self and hunger to be like Him cause the function of the cross—crucifixion—to become attractive. The long devastating years of abject bondage make freedom in the Lord Jesus priceless—the cost becomes as nothing to us! We begin to share (think of it!) the attitude of our Lord Jesus and of Paul. "For the joy that was set before him," the Lord Jesus "endured the cross" (Heb. 12:2). The attitude of the Apostle Paul became: "But God forbid that I should glory, save in the cross of our Lord Jesus Christ" (Gal. 6:14). "Let this mind [attitude] be in you, which was also in Christ Jesus" (Phil. 2:5).

Yes, we begin to glory in the cross, our very own freedom from all that enslaves, from all that would keep us from fellowship with our risen Lord. So we begin to take up our cross, our liberation, our personal finished work held in trust for us so long and patiently by the Holy Spirit. Talk about your trust funds!

And here is how we take up and bear our cross: Finally prepared by our needs, aware that our bondage was broken in Christ on Calvary, we definitely begin to rely on that finished work—we appropriate. Our attitude becomes: I gladly and willingly take, by faith in the facts, my finished work of emancipation that was established at Calvary; I reckon myself to be dead indeed to sin and alive to God in Christ. This is taking up one's cross. As we learn to do this, we begin to find these facts true in experience. The Holy Spirit brings that finished work of death and applies it to all of the old nature, which is thus held in the place of death—the death of Calvary. If and when we turn from the facts and begin to rely on anything or anyone else, including ourselves, self is released from the cross, as active and enslaving as ever. Through this process we are patiently taught to walk by faith, to maintain our attitude of reliance on the finished work of the cross.

Adolph Saphir wrote: "The narrow path, commencing with the cross—'Ye have died with Christ'—ending with the glory of the Lord Jesus, is the path on which the Lord draws near and walks with His disciples."

" 'Christ liveth in me.' The Lord within lives as the sole source of life. The old 'I' has no contribution he can make to Christian life and service; he can never be harnessed to the purposes of God. Death is his decreed portion. There cannot be two masters in our lives. If the old 'I' is in active possession of us then Christ cannot be. But if we gladly take hold of the great fact of redemption—'I have been crucified with Christ'—then Christ by His Spirit takes up the exercise of the function of life within us, and leads us as His bond-slaves (disciples), in the train of His triumph."

PROCESS OF DISCIPLESHIP

In the parable of the sower the seed sown "on the good ground are they, which in an honest and good heart, having heard the word, keep it, and bring forth fruit with patience" (Luke 8:15). The principle of growth is always "first the blade, then the ear, after that the full corn in the ear" (Mark 4:28). Therefore, "the husbandman waiteth for the precious fruit of the earth, and hath long patience for it" (James 5:7). As this clearly exemplifies, "he that believeth shall not make haste" (Isa. 28:16).

For most of us it has been a long season of growth from the tiny green blade up to the "full corn in the ear." So many seek to settle for this stage: saved, with heaven assured—plus a pacifying measure of Christian respectability, at least in church circles. Here we have the believer as a normal grain of wheat containing life inside a more or less shiny golden covering, in fellowship high up on the stalk with similar kernels of wheat. This is but a stage, not the goal. And, like middle age, this can be a dangerous stage—one of seeking a "much deserved" rest, of basking aimlessly in the fellowship of meetings, classes, etc., of ignoring or forgetting the struggles and growing pains of the tiny green blades down at one's feet and expecting and exhorting them to shape up and mature without delay.

This is all very cozy but costly, snug but sterile. "The seed corn may be beautiful, but it is hard. The germ of life is locked up within its shell and cannot get out. Therefore it produces nothing. Here is the reason why so many Christians, even preachers, are so unfruitful. Only one here and there is a soul winner. When the grain of corn is buried it dies, and that hard exterior surface softens and decays, in order to give nutriment to the young sprout, which would otherwise die and thus cause a crop failure. One must reckon himself dead to the hard, cold, selfish 'I' before the softening influence of the Holy Spirit can operate, qualifying the believer in the service of God. Many want to do God's work but are unable, because of the 'flesh' in their lives."

Our Father understands all this, and it is He who takes the initiative in the matter. He drops the seed of dissatisfaction into our hearts; He begins to show us that there is far more to this Christian life than just being saved and active for Him. And it is necessary for Him to engineer our exchange from carnal kernel Christians to fruitful fellowshipping disciples. From an infinite number of ways, He chooses the most effective for each individual's transition. And in the hand of the Husbandman, there is no fear, but freedom.

"We often come across Christians who are bright and clever, and strong and righteous; in fact, a little too bright, and a little too clever—there seems so much of self in their strength, and their righteousness is severe and critical. They have everything to make them saints, except . . . crucifixion, which would mold them into a supernatural tenderness and limitless charity for others. But if they are of the real elect, God has a winepress prepared for them, through which they will some day pass, which will turn the metallic hardness of their nature into gentle love, which Christ always brings forth at the last of the feast."

"Another parable put he forth unto them, saying, The kingdom of heaven is likened unto a man which sowed good seed in his field. . . . He that soweth the good seed is the Son of Man; the field is the world; the good seed are the children of the kingdom" (Matt. 13:24,37,38). The Lord of the harvest plants, or buries, Christians as seeds in a field, which is the world.

Through the Husbandman's patient and loving cultivation the grain of wheat high up on the stalk begins to fear being garnered alone and hungers to bring forth "much fruit" (John 12:24). Here is God's motivation for discipleship: that filial heart-hunger for fruit bearing. The believer finally pleads to be made fruitful at any cost, and then he hears the Lord say, "Verily, verily, I say unto you, Except a corn of wheat fall into the ground and die, it abideth alone: but if it die, it bringeth forth much fruit" (v. 24). "Whosoever shall lose his life for my sake and the gospel's, the same shall save it" (Mark 8:35). In loving response to this hunger the Holy Spirit silently and gently begins to loosen the grain from its comfortable bindings and supports in the ear. "When the fruit is brought forth, immediately he putteth in the sickle, because the harvest is come" (4:29). As a result, sooner or later the grain of wheat finds itself, not high up on the stalk, but dropped to the earth, into the cold and strange darkness. And still worse, the earth smears and injures that nice, shiny golden coat. Worst of all, the coat begins to disintegrate and fall to pieces. All that is not Christ, no matter how nice in appearance and profession, is revealed for what it is—just self.

There is a further stripping, right down to the germ of life, right on down until there is nothing left but Christ, who is our life. Down, down into death. Patience, grain of wheat: "Though he slay me, yet will I trust in him" (Job 13:15).

'Except it fall into the ground and die' . . .
   Can 'much fruit' come alone at such a cost?
Must the seed corn be buried in the earth,
   All summer joy and glory seemingly lost?
He buries still His seed corns here and there,
   And calls to deeper fellowship with Him
Those who will dare to share the bitter cup,
   And yet while sharing, sing the triumph hymn.

'Except it fall into the ground and die' . . . ?
   But what a harvest in the days to come;
When fields stand thick with golden sheaves of corn
   And you are sharing in the Harvest Home.
To you who 'lose your life,' and let it 'die,'
   Yet in the losing 'find' your life anew,
Christ evermore unveils His lovely face,
   And thus His mirrored glory rests on you.
                    —Selected.

When the believer takes up his cross for discipleship, the process of death begins to set in. The disciple finds himself a seed sown by the Son, planted in a home, office, hospital, church, parsonage or mission station. Whatever or wherever it is, there will be the death from which resurrection life follows. "For we which live are alway delivered unto death for Jesus' sake, that the life also of Jesus might be made manifest in our mortal flesh. So then death worketh in us, but life in you" (II Cor. 4:11,12). We need to enter deeply into the truth that Christ the beloved Son of the Father could not enter to the glory of heaven until He had first given Himself over to death. And this great truth, as it opens to us, will help us to understand how in our life, and in our fellowship with Christ, it is impossible for us to share His life until we have first in very deed surrendered ourselves every day to die to sin and self and the law and the world, and so to abide in the unbroken fellowship of discipleship with our crucified and risen Lord.

All the truths we have learned about the cross, of our death with Christ, of our death to sin with Him and of our conformity to death like the kernel of wheat falling into the ground to die, are preparatory to the overcoming life. They are the foundation of and fundamental to it.

REST

"There remaineth therefore a rest to the people of God. For he that is entered into his rest, he also hath ceased from his own works, as God did from his. Let us labour therefore to enter into that rest" (Heb. 4:9-11). So many of the life-giving truths in the Word consist of two intertwining halves that are inseparable. "Let us labour therefore to enter into that rest." As for labor, it is true that there is a great deal of struggling and searching and pleading and agonizing in the process of discovering and understanding truths fitted to our needs. And much of the same pathway is trod (or crawled) in an effort to appropriate and enter in. All this is not in vain; it is necessary. But it is not the key that opens the door to reality. Rest is the key to entering into rest!

In the important but exhausting labor process we come to see the needed truth; we become sure of our facts; we begin to realize something of what is ours in the Lord Jesus Christ. The appropriation of, the resting in, the reality must be on the basis of faith, not struggle and labor. We are told to reckon, to count on, what we now know to be true of us in Him as set forth in the Word. "In quietness and in confidence shall be your strength" (Isa. 30:15). We are told to quietly and steadily look to our Father in confident trust and thankfully receive that which He has given to us in His Son. "These wait all upon thee; that thou mayest give them their meat in due season. That thou givest them they gather: thou openest thine hand, they are filled with good" (Ps. 104:27,28).

Norman Grubb shares a good word on the principle of labor and rest: "Take as an example the learning of a foreign language. You are faced with a series of hieroglyphics in a book, you hear a medley of sounds around, which mean absolutely nothing. Yet you know that it is a language that can be learned. More than that, you have gone there to learn it. Now that is the first rung in the ladder of faith. However weak or waveringly, in your heart you do believe that you can and will get it. Otherwise, obviously you wouldn't try to learn it. So you plod on. Many a time faith and courage fail, the mind is weary and the heart is heavy, and you almost give up. But not quite. To give up is faith's unforgiveable sin. On you go at it. Months pass. It seems largely to go in one ear and out the other. Then—the length of time depends on the difficulty of the language and the ability and industry of the pupil of course—a miracle seems to happen. The day or period comes when, without your hardly realizing it, what you are seeking has found you; what you are trying to grasp has grasped you! You just begin automatically to speak the language, to think it, to hear it. What was an incomprehensible jumble of sounds without, has become an ordered language within the mind.

"So, in the spiritual labor of faith, the moment or period comes when we know. Every vestige of strain and labor is gone. Indeed, faith, as such, is not felt or recognized any more. The channel is lost sight of in the abundance of the supply. As we came to know that we were children of God by an inner certainty, a witness of the Spirit in our spirits; so now we come to know that the old 'I' is crucified with Christ, the new

'I' has Christ as its permanent life, spirit with Spirit have been fused into one; the branch grafted into the vine; the member joined to the body, the problem of abiding becomes as natural as breathing."

Thank God for the needs that just will not allow the hungry heart to stop short of finding them met in Him. It is necessary to remember a fundamental principle in the spiritual life: that God only reveals spiritual truths to meet spiritual needs. How many rest on the initial stage of the new birth: "Born again ... of incorruptible [seed] by the word of God" (I Pet. 1:23) and fail to press on to know "Begotten ... by the resurrection of Jesus Christ ... to an inheritance" (vv. 3,4).

Through the years the hungry-hearted believer finds that he has been brought a long way, and each step of the way has been personally experienced. This is reality which springs from faith founded on the facts of the Word. "The more clearly we enter by faith into objective truth, or what is true of us in Christ, the deeper, more experiential, and practical, will be the subjective work in us, and the more complete will be the manifestation of the moral effect in our life and character" (C.H.M.).

Yes, brought a long way, walking a step at a time, by faith: The rest of faith concerning our justification; the rest of faith concerning our acceptance; the rest of faith concerning our position in Christ Jesus; the rest of faith concerning our identification with Christ in death, resurrection and ascension. Each step established in the rest of faith brings us to the next one. Each must be settled before the next can be rested on.

It cannot be too strongly stated that unless the believer is firmly established in the steps of Romans

1-5, he cannot truly enter and rest on the truths of Romans 6-8, no matter how many special meetings and conferences he attends or so-called revivals he becomes involved in.

"Dr. James of Albany, who was used to bring hundreds into the deeper truths, declared that he usually found that 'failure in the higher stages of the Christian life was due to imperfect understanding and acceptance of the gospel of salvation in its fundamental principles.' It is a rare thing to be able to sit down and teach, because in most settings today one is limited to dealing with 'the first principles of the oracles of God,' and can go little further than the basic facts of the new birth. You cannot deepen spiritual life that is not there! You will only build askew if the foundations are not properly laid! A lack of appreciation of the wonder of a full salvation in Christ opens the door to every kind of overbalance and spells continual frustration and failure" (J. C. Metcalfe).

Often believers manage to trust God for truths they need, only to slip from grace over into the legal realm in seeking to produce the particular truth in their life or service. Once in possession of a truth, we are to rest—He will produce.

"In actual experience, when we have apprehended our deliverance through death with Christ, the self-life often appears more alive than ever! Just here God would have us stand firm (rest) upon His written Word. The increasing revelation proves the surrender to the cross to be real, because the Holy Spirit takes us at our word and reveals all that He has seen lying underneath—reveals it that it may be dealt with at the cross. Our part is to yield our wills, and take God's side against ourselves, whilst the Holy Spirit applies the death of the cross to all that is contrary to Him, that it may be really true that we who are of Christ have crucified the flesh with the affections and lusts (Gal. 5:24).

"The faith that receives from the hand of the Father is in two stages, and we are not to give up just because the struggle-and-labor phase does not produce the prize. 'According to your faith be it unto you.' And, do not let us forget, faith begins by being a labor (Heb. 4:11) or fight (I Tim. 6:12), although it is consummated in a rest (Heb. 4:3). That is to say, the first stage of faith is always the battle of taking hold by the will, heart, and intelligence of some truth or promise which is not real to us in experience, and declaring it to be ours in spite of appearances. We do not appear to be dead unto sin and alive unto God. We are told to believe it, and so we dare to do so and declare so. A thousand times, maybe, faith will be assaulted and fall: unbelief will say 'nonsense,' and we shall belie our declaration of faith; but the labor of faith means that we deliberately return to the assault. Once again we believe and declare it. This we persist in doing. As we thus follow in the steps of those who 'by faith and patience inherit the promises,' a new divine thing will happen within us. The Spirit will cooperate with our faith (as He is invisibly doing all the time), and to faith will be added assurance. Labor will be replaced by rest. The consummation of faith has been reached" (N. Grubb).

"True activity is that which springs out of, and is ever accompanied by, rest. It is only as we know what it is to be 'still,' that we are ready to 'go forward.' 'We rest on Thee, and in Thy Name we go' " (E. H.).

"Let us take care lest we get out of soul-rest in seeking further blessing. God cannot work whilst we are anxious, even about our spiritual experience. Let us take Him at His Word, and leave the fulfilment of it to Him."

HELP

For most of us, it is time to stop asking God for help. He didn't help us to be saved, and He doesn't intend to help us live the Christian life.

Immaturity considers the Lord Jesus a helper. Maturity knows Him to be life itself. Dr. J. E. Conant wrote: "Christian living is not our living with Christ's help, it is Christ living His life in us. Therefore that portion of our lives that is not His living is not Christian living; and that portion of our service that is not His doing is not Christian service; for all such life and service have but a human and natural source, and Christian life and service have a supernatural and spiritual source." Paul insisted, "For to me to live is Christ" (Phil. 1:21) and, "I can do all things through Christ" (4:13).

William R. Newell said, "Satan's great device is to drive earnest souls back to beseeching God for what God says has already been done!" Each of us had to go beyond the "help" stage for our new birth and thank Him for what He had already done on our behalf. God could never answer a prayer for help in the matter of justification. The same principle holds true for the Christian life. Our Lord Jesus waits to be wanted and to be all in us and do all through us. "For in him dwelleth all the fulness of the Godhead bodily. And ye are complete in him" (Col. 2:9,10).

God is not trusted, not honored, in our continually asking Him for help. In the face of "my God shall supply all your need according to his riches in glory by Christ Jesus" (Phil. 4:19), how can we beg for help? Our responsibility is to see in the Word all that is ours in Christ and then thank and trust Him for that which we need.

Sooner or later we must face up to what F. J. Huegel declares: "When a Christian's prayer life springs from a right position (a thorough adjustment to Christ in His death and resurrection), a vast change in procedure follows. Much of the mere begging type (though of course asking is always in order, for the Lord says, 'Ask and ye shall receive' [John 16:24]) gives away to a positive and unspeakably joyous appropriation. Much of our begging fails to register in heaven because it fails to spring from right relations with the Father in union with Christ in death and resurrection: in which position one simply appropriates what is already his. 'All things,' says the Apostle Paul, 'are your's. And ye are Christ's; and Christ is God's' (I Cor. 3:21,23)."

Since "without faith it is impossible to please him" (Heb. 11:6), we might consider several more strong but true statements to further clarify the attitude of faith that does please His heart.

"In our private prayers and in our public services," Dr. A. W. Tozer writes, "we are forever asking God to do things that He either has already done or cannot do because of our unbelief. We plead for Him to speak when He has already spoken and is at that very moment speaking. We ask Him to come when He is already present and waiting for us to recognize Him. We beg the Holy Spirit to fill us while all the time we are preventing Him by our doubts."

Dr. S. D. Gordon admonished: "When you are in the thick of the fight, when you are the object of attack, plead less and claim more, on the ground of the blood of the Lord Jesus. I do not mean ask God to give you victory, but claim His victory, to over-shadow you."

Watchman Nee startles many by saying, "God's way of deliverance is altogether different from man's way. Man's way is to try to suppress sin by seeking to overcome it; God's way is to remove the sinner. Many Christians mourn over their weakness, thinking that if only they were stronger all would be well. The idea that, because failure to lead a holy life is due to our impotence, something more is therefore de-manded of us, leads naturally to this false concep-tion of the way of deliverance. If we are preoccupied with the power of sin and with our inability to meet it, then we naturally conclude that to gain the vic-tory over sin we must have more power. 'If only I were stronger,' we say, 'I could overcome my violent outbursts of temper,' and so we plead with the Lord to strengthen us that we may exercise more self-control.

"But this is altogether wrong; this is not Chris-tianity. God's means of delivering us from sin is not by making us stronger and stronger, but by making us weaker and weaker. This is surely a peculiar way of victory, you say; but it is the Divine way. God sets us free from the dominion of sin, not by strengthen-ing our old man but by crucifying him; not by help-ing him to do anything but by removing him from the scene of action."

The believer does not have to beg for help. He does have to thankfully appropriate that which is already his in Christ, for, "the just shall live by faith" (Heb. 10:38). And dear old Andrew Murray encourages us with this: "Even though it is slow, and with many a stumble, the faith that always thanks Him—not for experiences, but for the promises on which it can rely—goes on from strength to strength, still increasing in the blessed assurance that God himself will perfect His work in us (Phil. 1:6)."

CULTIVATION

There can be little question concerning the importance of balance, so vital in the mechanical, physical, aesthetic and spiritual realms. Faulty balance often results in disintegration and possible devastation to the surrounding area.

Our self-life is out of balance—it is all one-sided. Like the universal Tea Party:

> I had a little tea party,
>   One afternoon at three;
> 'Twas very small, three guests in all,
>   Just I, myself and me.
>
> Myself ate up the sandwiches,
>   While I drank up the tea,
> 'Twas also I who ate the pie
>   And passed the cake to me.

Husbandman that He is, the beginning of God's cultivation of the hungry-hearted believer is downward. Patiently, persistently and painfully our Father digs down into the recesses of self, more and more fully revealing to us just what we are, and are not, in ourselves. His reason for this preparation is twofold: that the Lord Jesus might be free to manifest Himself in us and then through us for the sake of others—growing and sharing. "The Lord shall guide thee continually, and satisfy thy soul in drought, and make fat thy bones: and thou shalt be like a watered garden, and like a spring of water, whose waters fail not" (Isa. 58:11).

Each of us must be thoroughly cultivated before He can effectively cultivate others through us. It is not that there will be no service for us until we are spiritually mature but that most of our service on the way to maturity is for our own development, not so much that of others. At first the growing believer thinks, and would have others feel, that all his service is effective; but in time he comes to realize that the Lord is not doing so much through him as He is in him. Our Lord always concentrates on the greater need.

"Since the work of God is essentially spiritual, it demands spiritual people for its doing; and the measure of their spirituality will determine the measure of their value to the Lord. Because this is so, in God's mind the servant is more than the work. If we are going to come truly into the hands of God for His purpose, then we shall be dealt with by Him in such a way as to continually increase our spiritual measure. Not our interest in Christian work; our energies, enthusiasm, ambitions, or abilities; not our academic qualification, or anything that we are in ourselves, but simply our spiritual life is the basis of the beginning and growth of our service to God. Even the work, when we are in it, is used by Him to increase our spiritual measure" (anon.).

"It is a mistake to measure spiritual maturity merely by the presence of gifts. By themselves they are an inadequate basis for a man's lasting influence to God. They may be present and they may be valuable, but the Spirit's object is something far greater— to form Christ in us through the working of the cross. His goal is to see Christ inwrought in believers. So it is not merely that a man does certain things or speaks certain words, but that he is a certain kind of man. He himself is what he preaches. Too many want to preach without being the thing themselves, but in the long run it is what we are, and not simply what we do or say, that matters with God; and the difference lies in the formation of Christ within" (Watchman Nee).

We are not saved to serve, we are matured to serve. Only to the extent that cultivation reveals self for what it is are we in the position to assist others in their cultivation. We find out everyone else by first finding ourselves out. "As in water face answereth to face, so the heart of man to man" (Prov. 27:19). To counterbalance knowledge of self, our Father enables us to "grow in grace, and in the knowledge of our Lord and Saviour Jesus Christ" (II Pet. 3:18).

This is true not only concerning general service but also in the matter of our ministry of intercession. More than anything else the service of prayer for others necessitates a triune understanding—that of our Father, of ourselves and of others. "Praying for others can only flow from a heart at rest about itself, and knowing the value of the desires which it expresses for another. I could not be true or happy in praying otherwise" (Stoney). Paul wrote that he would "pray with my spirit—by the Holy Spirit that is within me; but I will also pray intelligently—with my mind and understanding" (I Cor. 14:15, Amplified).

So many of us, after having entered into some of the deeper realities of our Lord, seek to immediately pull or push others into this wonderful advancement; and then we wonder why they are so slow to learn and seemingly apathetic in their understanding and concern. We so easily forget the many years it took, and by what wandering wilderness ways our Lord had to traverse with us in order to bring us over Jordan and into Canaan.

"Moses had all the wisdom of the Egyptians, yet his idea of delivering Israel was to slay an Egyptian! He had to be trained in God's ways, having forty years in Midian, and when he was sent back to Egypt, God said for him not to trouble about Israel but to go directly to Pharaoh, the cause of their chains! God didn't train Israel at the first but a leader to lead Israel. God seeks to get leaders trained in the knowledge of His ways."

To the extent that we learn how our Father has had to handle us through the years will we understand how He would have us share with others. We must be cultivated to be cultivators. "It is injurious for one believer to be forcing another into 'blessing' which that soul may not be ready for. Forced advance really gives the enemy his opportunity to mislead, for those who try to rush on at the push of others cannot stand alone, nor bear the tests of their assumed positions" (J. Penn-Lewis).

Then, too, in all our service there is the proper motive to be fully considered. "Work should be regarded less with reference of its immediate results, or as to how it may affect this or that person; the great question is, will it, when sifted in His presence, be acceptable to Him? And this acceptability to Him is my reward: 'Wherefore we labour that, whether present or absent, we may be accepted of him' (II Cor. 5:9). One does not enough go forth to work in the joy and strength of one who comes out from his home to run his course. Many seem to droop because there are no grapes and are not happy unless they are doing.

Doing is right enough in itself, but the order ought to be from happiness to work, and not work to be happy. It is from the inner circle, the hive, the heart where Christ reigns, the only green spot, the fond enclosure—the sanctuary, that one should come forth to work. The quality of one's work depends on the nature of one's rest—and the rest should be like His own, known and enjoyed with Him. We have but small ideas of how our outward bears the color of our inward, and if our inward is not restful, there cannot be a rest-imparting service, however it may be attempted. . . . The greatest proof of our love for Christ is that we care for those who belong to Him; 'Lovest thou me? . . . Feed my sheep' [John 21:16]" (J. B. Stoney).

CONTINUANCE

When we first start out, hungry and zealous for Him, it is often imagined that extensive progress has been made when as yet we have barely begun. As our Lord takes us along through the years, it slowly dawns on us that there are vast, almost infinite, areas of development through which He must still lead us.

Many of these development areas are just plain desert—no spiritual activity, no service, little or no fellowship with Him or with others. What prayer there is has to be forced and is sometimes dropped altogether for months at a time. Bible study finally grinds to a halt; everything seems to add up to nothing. It is during these necessary times that the believer often feels that God has ceased to carry out His part and that there is little or no use in seeking to continue on. And yet there is a hunger deep within that will not allow him to quit. "The foundation of God standeth sure, having this seal, The Lord knoweth them that are his" (II Tim. 2:19).

Are we to love and trust and respond to Him only when He seems to be "blessing" us? What sort of love is that? Self-love? Our Father strips everything away from time to time in order to give us the opportunity of loving and trusting and responding to Him just because He is our Father. He knows what the cross is going to mean in our lives. He knows the death-march that lies ahead of us in order that there may be resurrection life. He knows the barren, bleeding hearts beyond to whom He must minister through us—hence He is going to bring us to the place where we don't care what happens, He is all that matters!

"Sonship is something more than being born again. It represents growth into fulness. It is quite a good thing to be a babe while babyhood lasts, but it is a bad thing to be a babe when that period is past. This is the condition of many Christians. While sonship is inherent in birth, in the New Testament sense sonship is the realization of the possibilities of birth. It is growth to maturity. So the New Testament has a lot to say about growing up, leaving childhood and attaining unto full stature. With this growth comes the greater fulness of Christ and the abundant wealth unto which we are saved. It is a matter not so much of that from which we are saved as of that unto which we are saved" (T. Austin-Sparks).

In the beginning we are mainly taken up with the externals of our Christian life, and the Lord allows this for a time. Then, in order to get us and our externals out of the way so that the Lord Jesus Christ can be our all, our Father begins to take away much of what we thought we had. Here begins the long cross-centered transition from "do" to "be."

All this paradoxical progress—the way up being down—has a strong tendency to make us feel that the Lord is not taking us on. This is simply a weapon of the enemy, easily parried by letting God be God in the scriptural knowledge that He is our Father.

"It is true that God does take up those who are not worthy and permits them to speak His words years before they fully understand their import; but He does not wish any of us to stop there. We may go on in that way for awhile, but is it not true that, from the time when He begins in us His work of formation through discipline and chastening, it growingly dawns on us how little in fact we knew of the true meaning of what we had been saying and doing? He intends that we should reach the place where we can speak, with or without manifest gifts, because we are the thing we say. For in Christian experience the spiritual things of God are less and less outward, that is, of gift, and more and more inward, of life. In the long run it is the depth and inwardness of a work that counts. As the Lord himself becomes more and more to us, other things—yes, and this must include even His gifts—matter less and less. Then, though we teach the same doctrine, speak the same words, the impact on others is very different, manifesting itself in an increasing depth of the Spirit's work within them also" (Watchman Nee).

His relentless processing will discourage and baffle us if we simply want heaven when we die. But if we want what He wants, all that we are taken through, including the desert, will encourage us. Thus we will continue because we know that He ever continues to work in and through us that which He began and finished on our behalf in our Lord Jesus Christ.

"If our hearts are really true to Him we may be assured He will lead us on in the knowledge of Himself just as fast as we are able to advance. He knows how much we can take in, and He does not fail to minister to us the very food that is suitable to our present need. We may sometimes feel inclined to be impatient with ourselves because we do not make more rapid progress, but we have to learn to trust the Lord with our spiritual education. If our eyes are upon Him, and we follow with simple hearts as He leads us, we shall find that He leads us by a right way and brings us through all the exercises we need in order to form our souls in the appreciation of Himself, and of all those blessed things which are brought to pass in Him. We have to trust His love all through, and to learn increasingly to distrust ourselves" (C. A. Coates).

Paul writes to us, as he did to Timothy: "Thou therefore, my son, be strong in the grace that is in Christ Jesus. And the things that thou hast heard of me among many witnesses, the same commit thou to faithful men, who shall be able to teach others also. Thou therefore endure hardness, as a good soldier of Jesus Christ" (II Tim. 2:1-3). We rejoice with you as you continue in Him. "The Lord is faithful, who shall stablish you" (II Thess. 3:3).

Back to the Bible is a nonprofit ministry dedicated to Bible teaching, evangelism and edification of Christians worldwide.

If we may assist you in knowing more about Christ and the Christian life, please write to us without obligation:

Back to the Bible
P. O. Box 82808
Lincoln, NE 68501